Governing and Managing Church Schools

An introductory guide

David W. Lankshear

The National Society
Leading Education with a Christian Purpose
Church House Publishing

National Society/Church House Publishing
Church House
Great Smith Street
London
SW1P 3NZ

ISBN 0 7151 4921 0

Published 2000 by the National Society (Church of England) for Promoting Religious Education and Church House Publishing.

Acknowledgements

I would like to express my appreciation for the advice and support of my colleagues Canon John Hall and Daphne Griffith throughout the preparation of this book. On the legal dimension the comments of Nick Richens of Lee Bolton & Lee have been invaluable, as has the contribution of Peter Williams and his colleagues from the Welsh dioceses to those parts of the book which refer to the situations for Church in Wales schools.

Cover design by Julian Smith

Printed in England by The Cromwell Press Ltd, Trowbridge, Wiltshire

Contents

Introduction

One of the major characteristics of Anglicanism is its generous and open commitment to education. Most Anglican parishes offer opportunities for children, young people and adults to learn more about the faith and about themselves. Anglican churches and halls are often used to host educational and cultural activities. Wherever the Anglican Church flourishes, it has created schools and universities or colleges. Usually these initiatives welcome pupils and students regardless of their own faith background.

As a reader of this book, you are almost certain to be involved in this Anglican enterprise of education. You may be a governor, a teacher, a member of staff, or a parent at an Anglican school. You may be, or have been, a pupil or student at an Anglican school or college. You may have been to Sunday school, scouts, guides, a playgroup or an adult education class run in church premises, probably partly funded or subsidized by the church. There can be few people in England and Wales who have not been in contact at some point in their lives with the Anglican Church's educational work.

Probably you are now making, or planning to make, a significant contribution to this work as a governor or teacher in an Anglican school. This book serves as an introduction to the world of Church schools. It is designed to help teachers, governors and other staff understand how their work fits into the vision of a Church school as a whole. It cannot be a comprehensive guide. It contains, however, a number of routes into the most comprehensive resource for Church schools that has ever been produced by the National Society in the whole of its 200-year history. The accompanying web site is available to every Church of England and Church in Wales school on payment of a modest annual subscription. The site has been developed to help you with detailed and up-to-the-minute information on all aspects of the management of Church schools. Each of the major sections of this booklet is also an introduction to a section of the web site. The route into that specific section of the site is provided at the end of each section of the booklet. This booklet and the web site are intended to complement and support the help, advice and training available to you from your diocese.

Every diocese has a Diocesan Director of Education (DDE) who works with a professional team and a Diocesan Board of Education (DBE) to support the work of schools and colleges in the diocese. If you do not know the name of your Diocesan Director of Education, your school will be able to give you this information or you can obtain it from the National Society's open web site.

Before reading the main sections on different aspects of Church schools, it is important to put today's Church schools in their historic context. Many of our schools have their roots in the generosity and foresight of Christians at the end of the eighteenth and the beginning of the nineteenth centuries. At this time there was a great movement to provide formal education for all children in England and Wales, including initiatives taken by SPCK, the Sunday School Movement, the Welsh Trust, the Gruffydd Jones' Circulating Schools and some enlightened landowners who provided schools for the poor of their parishes. This movement was given a national focus by two great Church societies: the British and Foreign Schools Society acted on behalf of the Free Churches and the National Society on behalf of the Church of England. It is not insignificant that this booklet is published by the same National Society, which continues to make the support of Church schools a major aspect of its mission.

Between 1800 and 1870 most of the schools founded to provide elementary education for the children of the poor were established by the Churches, albeit with some help from the state in the form of government grants to the two societies. Only after the Education Act of 1870 did it become possible for schools to be organized entirely by, initially, School Boards and, subsequently, Local Education Authorities. Over the years since 1870 the partnership between church and state has developed through a series of changes and reforms that reflect the ever-increasing demands for higher standards of educational achievement for all our children. At the time of writing, the most recent reform has been the School Standards and Framework Act 1998. The debates around the passage of this piece of legislation contain an important reaffirmation of the partnership in education between the church and the state.

Subsequent to the passage of the Act, the work of Anglican schools was debated at the meeting of the Church of England General Synod in November 1998. Although some members were critical of particular events or policies in individual Church schools, no one spoke against the Church's involvement in education or the existence of Church schools within the maintained system in this country. At the end of the debate the Synod passed the following resolution (see p. 4) without a single member voting against it.

That this Synod, believing that Church Schools stand at the centre of the Church's mission to the nation:

(a) strongly urge:

(i) Diocesan Synods, in the light of the School Standards and Framework Act, to review the resources available to Diocesan Boards of Education to enable them to be involved in all aspects of statutory education;

(ii) each PCC to discuss how it can serve all schools in the parish;

(iii) each PCC to commit itself to the greatest possible active support for Church schools in its area;

(iv) each Deanery Synod to consider how it can assist parishes in providing active support for Church schools which serve several parishes within its area;

(b) welcome the opportunities for Church schools to move to the voluntary aided category and encourages dioceses to support governors in so doing, where appropriate; and

(c) invite the Archbishops' Council to review the achievements of Church schools and to make proposals for the future development of Church Schools and Church colleges of further and higher education.

In the Autumn of 1999 the Bench of Bishops of the Church in Wales considered the contribution of Anglican schools to the work of the Church in the province. They approved the following statement:

The Bench of Bishops of the Church in Wales:

- supports the continuing contribution of the Church in Wales to the dual system of education in England and Wales;
- acknowledges the role of the National Society in enabling this support to be effective;
- encourages the Church's Provincial and Diocesan Education Officers to develop their work in statutory education in cooperation with Local Education Authorities and the National Assembly;
- welcomes the new opportunities presented to the Church in Wales by the School Standards and Framework Act 1998;
- supports, subject to the decision of the Diocesan Trust, any Voluntary Controlled school wishing to change its status to that of a Voluntary Aided school;
- maintains that Church schools are central to the Church's mission to the nation;
- invites the whole church community at parochial, deanery, diocesan and provincial level to share in this vision and to promote teaching as a Christian vocation.

This resolution represents an enthusiastic endorsement and affirmation of the role of Church schools and all who work in them. It is the National Society's hope that this book and the accompanying web site will help you to enjoy the work that you do in the Church's schools.

Broadly, the book lays out the principles; the web site provides greater detail and the legal references. For example, the section on curriculum contains statements about the different requirements for Religious Education in different categories of school. If you wish, you can use the web site to check where these requirements are detailed in the law of education. The web site will also alert you to other issues related to Religious Education, which could affect the situation in a particular school.

Education law changes – between 1986 and 1998 there were thirteen Education Acts. The principles on which Anglican schools are organized are more constant. That is why the book deals with these principles and the web site deals with the law. The web site will be regularly updated to ensure that it reflects the current state of the law of education. You should be able to access the site through your school's computer, or on your own if you have access to the web and pay your own subscription.

A word of warning

No publication, however sophisticated, can cover every event and every incident. These materials are not a substitute for seeking advice from your diocese or the National Society. What the materials can do is to help you deal with the routine events and frame your questions more precisely.

Further changes in education law, local practice or even mistakes – we all make them – may mean that you feel that some of the material could be improved or an emphasis changed. It is important that you let us know about such items. We do not give incorrect or misleading information deliberately. We want to ensure that these tools to help you are as accurate as possible. You can help us to help you and others by letting us know what you think. We are bound to publish material based on the best legal advice we can obtain. There are times when local customs have grown up which are effective, but which do not reflect exactly the standard interpretation of the law. In such cases we are bound to point this out if asked about the matter. Within this material we use only examples that reflect our lawyers' advice.

If you wish to contact us you can write to us at:

The National Society
Church House
Great Smith Street
London, SW1P 3NZ

Telephone: 020 7222 1672
Fax: 020 7233 2592
Email: info@natsoc.c-of-e.org.uk

We hope you find the material useful in your work.

The Children Come First

A Church school is, or should be, the model of a Christian community. That is, a community that places the service of others, in the name of Christ, above all other considerations. It is a truism to state that schools are all about children. Truisms, however often repeated, are nevertheless true. The most important people in a school are the children. What best serves the needs of the children and their education should drive everything that happens in the school.

Every child is a unique human being made in the image of God. A Church school will seek to serve children because they are unique, made in God's image and beloved by him. In practical matters this leads to some tensions which will be explored in detail in the following pages, particularly in the sections on admissions, discipline and exclusions. But the principle is clear and must be known and understood by every adult working in or for the school.

No adult is beyond the reach of God's love, although many, sadly, turn away from him. If this is true for adults, how much more true must it be for children! This is not to adopt a starry-eyed view of childhood. Children can behave like little devils.

What adults working in schools must fully understand and witness in their attitudes and behaviour is that, even when children are behaving like devils, they are still within the scope of God's love and are still of great worth as human beings made in God's image. Christ's challenge to 'love one another as I have loved you' is a key text for all working in schools.

Having made some sweeping statements about the importance and worth of all children, we must now turn to some of the detailed aspects of the life of the school which affect them most. Some of these set up direct contradictions with the preceding paragraphs.

Admissions

Every school must have an admissions policy. This policy must be published in the school's brochure of information for parents. This has been a legal requirement for all schools since the Education Act 1980. Unfortunately, for a number of years after the 1980 act school rolls fell and for many schools the real policy was 'If the child's parents wish it to attend our school, it is in'. In recent years many schools have come under pressure for space. There have been school closures and a rise in the birth rate. There has been a government policy on the reduction of class sizes at Key Stage 1. As a result, many schools have found that they now have to use a policy which was created some time ago and which may not work effectively. An admissions policy determines which children will enter the school. It also determines which children will not gain a place. Here lies the tension with what has been said in the introduction to this chapter. If every child is within the scope of the love of God, how can a Church school become involved in selecting which children it will serve? This is a tension with which the governors have to live. It can be pleasant to know that your school is over-subscribed, but with that feeling must go the frustration of having to turn children away.

In Voluntary Aided and Foundation schools the admissions policy is a matter for the governing body. The governors determine the policy and then make the decisions based upon it. In this work they may have the assistance of the head teacher or other members of staff but the policies are theirs and the decisions are theirs.

If they wish to change the policy they must consult with the LEA and the governing bodies of other Voluntary Aided and Foundation schools that could be affected. They should also take into account the effect of the change on other local schools. This can best be done through the local Admissions Forum, where it exists.

In Voluntary Controlled schools it is the LEA which is responsible for admissions. The LEA will determine the policy and make the decisions. If there are to be changes, however, the LEA must consult the governing body about its proposals. In many cases the admissions policy adopted by the LEA recognizes the importance of denominational elements in the admission criteria.

In law the governing body and the LEA should consult each other every year about the admissions policy in a school. In practice, detailed consultations only happen when changes are being considered. At the time of writing this book there was no experience of the work of Admissions Forums available from which to provide detailed advice about their impact. For up-to-date information on Admissions Forums, please see the National Society's web site. Your local diocese will also be able to provide you with information about your local Admissions Forum.

The key factor in any review of the admissions procedure in the school is the number of places available. Unfortunately, there is some confusion about the way in which this can be calculated, because different parts of the law of education have, for different purposes, produced varying ways of calculating the overall capacity of the school. There are two figures of key significance: the school's capacity and the number that the governors indicate is their intended admissions limit for the year. In theory these two numbers should relate closely. If there are seven year-groups in the school, the number it is intended to admit should be the total capacity of the school divided by seven. In reality it is rarely as simple as that. In the first instance the government has introduced legislation designed to ensure that no child at Key Stage 1 is taught in a class of more than thirty. This means that a school must plan for its Key Stage 1 classes not to exceed this size. Mixed classes may be larger than thirty provided the majority of pupils in the class are at Key Stage 2. This legislation provides a constraint on planning and school organization. For schools where there is already more than one year-group in a class this may not be difficult, but where the tradition has been a single year-group in each class, parents may be resistant to changes in school organization. Governors wishing to review their admissions arrangements need to be clear on how the issue of school and class size may constrain their options.

How should governors set about developing or reviewing their school's admissions policy?

The first advice is, *seek help*.

Your Diocesan Education Office will be able to provide good advice based on years of experience in helping schools with such policies. Having ensured that there is help available to clarify the wording and avoid the dangers of ambiguous or misleading phrases, the governors must then establish the principles on which they will work.

There are two distinct views of the purposes of a Church school:

- One argues that the school should give first priority to the children of parents who are active members of the faith community.
- The second argues that the school should give priority to serving the children of the local community, regardless of the faith commitment of the parents.

Both are strong reasons for being a Church school.

There are many Anglican schools whose policies reflect one or other of these priorities. There are also Anglican schools that seek to hold both approaches together by allocating some of their places on a geographical and some on a church basis.

Whichever philosophy the governors espouse, there are constraints and problems associated with finding the appropriate words in which to frame the policy. There are also some general principles and rules.

- A good policy enables parents to see clearly where they stand. Clarity of wording is important.
- A good policy enables governors to draw a clear line between those children they will admit and those they will not.
- Unless the policy makes it clear that some other rule applies, the order in which the categories are listed is the order in which they must be applied.
- Wherever possible, statements made by parents should be verified by external evidence.
- Governors need to be able to produce the evidence that they have used to arrive at their judgements if the parents appeal against their decision.

The review of the policy by the governors is only the beginning of the process. They must consult with the LEA about their proposals. They should also seek the views of parents. Having carried out the consultation and approved the final version of the policy, the governors should then turn to their admissions application form. As far as possible this should follow the format used in the LEA in general, but it should also ensure that the governors collect from the parents all the information they will reasonably need in order to apply the admissions criteria. A good test is to go through the criteria and ask yourself, 'Where, in our application form, do we find the information needed for each criteria? Where are we given the names and addresses of those who will provide the references? Is there space for the parents to give us all the information we need? Is the form clear?'

When the governors have approved the application form, all parents who have already applied for places in the years for which the new policy will apply should be contacted and invited to review their application in the light of the new policy. They should be given reasonable time to do this. It is often helpful if a member of the staff of the school can offer assistance to parents who need help with the task.

Timetable for applications

Within the information provided to parents there should be a clear indication of the timetable for the decision-making process. Local schools working through the Admissions Forum may have agreed this, or it may have been left to individual schools to decide for themselves.

> The timetable for the admissions process should ensure that all children are well prepared to enter their new school.
>
> This implies that all children, including those admitted on appeal, should know that they will be coming to the school in time to take part in the pre-entry visiting programme that most schools organize to ensure smooth transfer or entry into school.

In many primary schools the timetable for applications is complicated by a pattern of entry into school that has children in the same year-group starting school at different points in the school year. Governors should decide which children are to be admitted to school as members of the same year-group at the same time, regardless of their actual start date. This should ensure that the criteria are applied fairly to the whole year-group. The decisions should usually be taken a clear term before the first children are scheduled to start school. This allows half a term for appeals to be resolved and half a term for the induction programme to take place.

This implies that parents have to apply for places at least one and a half terms before the first children in their child's year-group are admitted. This is not a problem for secondary schools, but it can be quite difficult for primary schools. Primary schools need to ensure that, once a good pattern is established, their practice is consistent and well known in the area.

The detailed decision-making process will be undertaken by a small group of governors acting with the authority of the whole governing body. They will need all the evidence available to them and they should act carefully to ensure that they consistently apply the policy approved by the whole governing body. They must not alter that policy during the decision-making process, even if they come to the conclusion that it needs further review. They must not use evidence that they have not been given formally. For example, in a small community it is possible that some members of the panel will know some of the families whose applications they are considering. Governors must be careful to avoid being influenced by this personal knowledge.

As soon as possible after the sub-committee has made its decisions, these should be communicated to the parents. The letter to unsuccessful applicants should include details of their rights of appeal and the timetable for such appeals. Successful applicants, particularly at secondary school level, should be asked to confirm their acceptance of the place.

Appeals

No over-subscribed school should feel inhibited from making decisions because of the existence of appeals procedure. For the appeals system to work properly, the governors of the school must also be undertaking their own responsibilities effectively. Having admitted those children whom they believe best match their published criteria, governors need to view any appeals as a useful independent check on their work.

Since admissions appeals panels were first introduced in the Education Act 1980, their constitution has gradually been changed so that they are now entirely independent of the school. Admissions appeals panels are usually convened on behalf of the governing body by the LEA or the diocese. Sometimes the clerk to the governors acts as convenor. There will be an established local practice which should be checked with the local school.

Appeals panels have two distinct issues to consider as they hear an appeal. Have the governors correctly administered their published policy in this case? Could the school provide a place for this child without distorting the good use of educational resources represented by the school's current organization and staffing levels? This second issue is a matter of balance between the parents' request for their child to be added to the school roll and the governors' explanation of the impact on the school of a further admission.

The appeals panel needs to hear all the appeals for places in a particular school before they decide to admit any child on the basis that this admission would, on balance, not have an excessively adverse effect on the use of educational resources in the school. If the panel feels that the school could admit two more pupils without undue problems, they must then decide which two of the pupils whose parents have appealed will receive the places. They can only do this after they have heard all the appeals.

While the appeals panel is a formal independent body, its hearings are usually informal and designed to put both parents and governors at their ease.

Nursery admissions – a special case

Everything that has been discussed about admissions so far applies to children entering school at or shortly before statutory school age. If the school has a nursery class this raises different issues. There may be historic agreements about admissions to the nursery entered into at the time that it was agreed that one would be created at the school. These may allocate a certain proportion of places to children nominated by the Local Authority Social Services department, for example. Within the Local Authority Early Years plan these historic agreements may have been reviewed or superseded. Where there are no special criteria in existence resulting from such constraints, the governors are free to establish their own. In practice it is almost impossible to sustain an admissions policy for the nursery which is different from that of the school in general. Parents do not accept statements which attempt to make it clear that a place in the nursery does not guarantee a place in the school. In one respect, however, the law is different. Parents have no right of appeal over the governors' decision not to admit their child to the nursery.

Attendance

Every child should attend school on every day that the school is open unless they are too ill to do so or there is an urgent need for them to be elsewhere. If a child is not at school an explanation should be provided by a parent for its absence. In these days when there is great concern for the safety of children it is helpful if such an explanation is given to the school either before the absence, in the case of such things as hospital appointments, or at the beginning of the absence, if a child is ill. If parents establish a pattern of informing the school before or at the start of an absence, then the school is in a good position to identify incidents of truancy and also the rare incidents that give rise to concern about the child's safety.

There are several possible causes of truancy and schools will need to be alert to incidents and prepared to take the necessary action to deal with the causes. This will need all the adults involved to work together in the interests of the child concerned. One or more of the following causes may cause truancy:

- problems at school with teachers or other adults;
- problems at school with pupils;
- problems at home;
- peer pressure;
- attraction of activities outside school.

If the school is to take positive action to reduce truancy it will need to be able to identify the causes of each individual's truancy and deal with them as far as this lies within the power of the staff. In extreme cases a child may need to change school or have a special regime of support created to enable him or her to make a return to school. The longer truancy is allowed to run on undetected or unchecked, the more difficult will be the child's return to school.

The above paragraphs have been written on the assumption that truancy is about missing whole days or sessions. A subsidiary pattern of truancy occurs in some schools, where pupils miss certain lessons, perhaps taking advantage of split sites or movement between buildings to avoid the most disliked subjects or teachers. Such truancy is best prevented by careful checking of registers at the beginning of lessons to ensure that the whole class is present and taking action if pupils are not where they are expected to be.

In recent years there has been much pressure on schools to take action to reduce the incidence of truancy and unauthorized absence. Only head teachers can authorize absence. On some occasions they may be approached to authorize absence so that children can take part in family holidays. This provision is intended to enable parents who cannot take their annual holiday during school holidays to have a holiday with their children. In recent years anxiety has been expressed about the abuse of this provision. Head teachers should seek to encourage parents to use the school holidays as far as possible, so that absence from school is minimized. This is essential, for while presence at school does not guarantee learning, absence from school certainly reduces it.

Discipline

The word discipline has come to have several meanings in common usage. Anyone becoming involved in a school will need to reflect on what it means in the context of a school. It is sometimes used instead of classroom control. We hear people talk about teachers having good discipline, meaning that they are able to exercise good control in the classroom. Again, the word is used to describe the standards of behaviour demonstrated by the pupils. 'The school is well disciplined' is an example of that type of usage.

Every school governing body must adopt a school discipline policy. The policy should have at least two distinct aims:

- to create an orderly environment in which teachers and pupils can work effectively;
- to establish an understanding of the need for self-discipline within pupils.

These two aims are mutually compatible, but they are not the same.

It is really a misnomer to refer to a school discipline policy. Any policy that focuses only on discipline will fail. An effective policy must include not only a clear understanding of what will happen when things go wrong but also a clear statement of how the school will react when things go well.

It is as important, in most cases, for good to be seen to be rewarded as it is for wrong to be seen to be punished.

The policy must relate to the school ethos statement; in Anglican schools, therefore, it will reflect Christian principles. Within the policy will be a clear statement of how the school will provide an experience of forgiveness and reconciliation when things have gone wrong. This may not be easy to sustain for those children who find conforming to the rules of the school difficult.

All the adults involved with the school must understand the school's policy and apply it as consistently as possible. Teachers will take the lead on this, but everyone who has contact with the pupils will have a contribution to make. A key group will be the dinner supervisors. Opportunities for providing them with training about their role in the policy and their work with the pupils will be limited, but are vital if there is to be consistency of practice throughout the day.

Another area in which it is hard to establish consistency is the reward system. Too often praise and encouragement come to those who achieve in absolute terms in classroom work, sport or music. Somewhere there must be opportunities for rewarding pupils who do their best, not because they are top but because they have surpassed their previous best achievement. A challenge to many schools may be 'How do we encourage and reward our well-behaved triers?' One means of doing this is to make constructive and imaginative use of Records of Achievement.

Many schools have found it helpful to agree certain basic statements about the standards of behaviour expected in the school, together with sanctions that will be applied if these standards are not met. These statements are then well publicized around the school in the expectation that this will promote consistency of behaviour and response. In most schools where this has been tried, it has been found to be helpful. There are difficulties with this approach, however. It works well for most pupils, most of the time. Within any school community there are occasions when a pupil arrives at school in a very disturbed state, or becomes very disturbed by what he or she experiences in school. For these children conforming to the basic rules becomes impossible. In such cases action needs to be taken swiftly to resolve the situation. A disturbed child needs to be taken out of the class setting and given help and support to enable them to return in a better frame of mind. Action like this does not condone bad behaviour, it seeks to prevent it. Swift preventive action also avoids other pupils perceiving any unfairness in the application of the general rules.

By the time the pupils leave school they should have developed into self-disciplined adults who understand and accept that there have to be some constraints on behaviour in a civilized society. The school's discipline policy should have this as one of its goals. Governors should be able to identify how that goal will be achieved. One of the elements of such a policy will be to give pupils responsibility in a safe environment where failure is not a total disaster but an experience from which to learn.

There are some specific elements within a discipline policy that need to be addressed in more detail.

1. *Exclusions*: The law allows for pupils to be excluded from school in extreme cases. There is considerable evidence that schools are using this power more frequently. It is not clear that this is always the result of extremely bad behaviour that could not have been foreseen or prevented. Governors have a

specific role in the exclusion process. A group of governors may be asked to hear an appeal against exclusion. It is essential, therefore, that governors do not discuss the circumstances of an individual incident outside such an appeal hearing. This is to ensure that any governor who is asked to sit on an appeal panel has not prejudged the situation. When hearing an appeal it is essential that the governors seek advice from the LEA or the diocese about their powers and the conduct of the appeal.

2. *Corporal punishment*: This is against the law and should not feature in any discipline policy for a maintained school.

3. *Detention*: Pupils may be kept back after school as a punishment but only after the parents have been given notice that the pupil will be late home. Inevitably, this means that any detention can only take place some time after the incident that has led to this form of punishment.

4. *Home/School agreements* have now become a standard requirement for all schools. They have two specific contributions to make to a discipline policy: they make the basis of the policy clear to all parents at the time when the pupil enters the school; and they provide a basis for further discussion and agreements if the pupil's behaviour within school is being discussed with the parents. This second purpose is particularly important when a pupil is either in difficulties or has been excluded for a short period and is being prepared for re-entry into school.

5. *Bullying* is a particularly difficult problem to handle successfully. It involves at least three groups of people: the bully, the victim and the bystander. A discipline policy will contain provisions for dealing with all forms of bullying, from physical assault to name calling and social exclusion. It will address how perpetrators are dealt with, victims supported and

bystanders encouraged to be more active in the creation of good relationships between everyone in the community.

6. *Racism* is a particularly unpleasant form of bullying. Every Church school should have a policy that actively addresses racism. This must include presenting positive images of the multi-racial aspects of our society as well as details of the way in which racist incidents will be handled.

Child protection

There is no more important issue within a school than the physical, emotional, intellectual and spiritual care and safety of the children.

Physical care and safety

The school will have a number of measures in place designed to ensure that the school is a safe place for children to be. Every adult who has substantial, unsupervised access to the pupils must be prepared to accept that they will be subject to police clearance under arrangements put in place by the LEA. This is one of the basic precautions created to ensure that no one who has demonstrated that they might be a danger to children has access to them within the school context.

Every adult entering the school premises will be asked to comply with the security arrangements that the school has in place. These will probably include signing in and out and wearing an identity badge while on the premises. The school entrance will be clearly signed from every point of access to the school grounds and all visitors will be asked to report to the secretary's office or other reception point before attempting to visit any other part of the school. Schools in areas where there is deemed to be a higher than normal level of risk will also have other measures in place. Detailed advice on these matters is available to governors and school managers from both the DfEE (or Welsh Assembly) and the LEA.

Physical safety is not just a matter of protecting pupils from attack by adults. It has many other aspects. The school will seek to ensure that all its activities are conducted in a safe manner, with appropriate precautions in place for the activity being undertaken. This includes the basic assumption that there is always an appropriate level of adult supervision. Governors will have adopted policies, usually on the advice of their LEA, which set appropriate standards in these areas.

A further aspect of physical safety is safety from other pupils. There is much public concern over bullying in schools. The governors will need to be satisfied that policies which they have approved are in place and being observed to combat bullying wherever it may arise. No school can ever afford to be complacent in this area. All schools need active policies which both deal with incidents when they arise and are designed to prevent their occurrence.

Emotional care and safety

This section leads naturally on from the previous paragraph. The problem with bullying is that it not only has an affect at the physical level, but also creates emotional damage. Nowhere is this more evident than when there is a racist content to the bullying. In some instances of bullying there is no physical content; the impact is almost totally emotional. Its symptoms are name-calling, social ostracism, sarcasm and personal comments or jokes. This type of bullying can be difficult to counter once it takes hold in a group, class or school. Schools must be active in prevention by always providing a clear example of good interpersonal relationships and actively promoting good relations between all children in the school, whatever their age, background, size, ability etc.

Preventing the emotional damage caused by bullying, however, is not the end of the school's responsibilities. Schools need to provide a safe and secure place in which children can work through issues that are distressing or worrying them.

Intellectual care and safety

Schools should be places where ideas are explored and individual differences valued. This implies that pupils must be safe to explore their own ideas. They should be able to do so in an atmosphere which may reject the idea or challenge the pupil to reconsider or explore the consequences of adopting the idea as part of their beliefs, but which never rejects the pupil because of the idea that they are exploring. This sounds rather a complex concept. Two examples will make the idea clear.

1. An eleven-year-old boy was present at an act of worship which included a presentation based on Genesis 1. At lunchtime he was heard to say to his teacher, 'You don't believe all this rubbish about God making the world in seven days, do you?' Some of his friends reacted with a display of shock at this expression of heresy in a Church school. The teacher accepted the comment and required the boy to take his expressed opinion seriously by responding with, 'What do you think?' There followed a lively discussion with the group, which explored some of the possible interpretations of the story.

2. A thirteen-year-old, in the course of a class discussion, makes an overt but possibly unintentional racist statement. The teacher in response makes it clear that there are people in the class who would be offended by the remark and asks the pupil to explain why they would be offended. Having been given the opportunity to think through the issue, the pupil is then asked to rephrase the statement in a way that is not

racist. Care is then taken to ensure that the other pupils in the group accept the rephrasing. The idea is rejected; the pupil is not. If the pupil persists in making racist statements, then that is dealt with within the context of the school's policy for dealing with racist behaviour. The principle here being that pupils are given the chance to withdraw from unthinking offensive statements or ideas.

Another aspect of intellectual safety relates to that particular aspect of peer pressure or bullying which focuses on a pupil's ability or lack of it. This is most often stereotyped as mockery of those who fail to learn as quickly as their peers or fail to acquire a sporting skill as easily. This is only one manifestation of this form of peer persecution. It can also manifest itself in mockery of those who learn easily or who show real interest or enthusiasm for the material being learned. Being mocked for what you can do is as difficult to deal with as being mocked for what you cannot. Schools need to guard against the development of either of these forms of bullying. This can be done by creating an atmosphere in which everyone is valued and where pupils undertake such a range of different activities that everyone experiences success and failure and learns to come to terms appropriately with both.

Spiritual care and safety

Schools have a responsibility for the spiritual development of their pupils. This does not just apply to those who are being brought up in the particular part of the Anglican tradition represented by the local parish. It is proper that within a school context they should be introduced to forms of spirituality which are outside their previous experience. There is a caveat, however. It is not appropriate to insist that pupils take part in activities that are contrary to the beliefs in which they are being raised or to which they hold. They can learn about how other people express their spirituality. They may discuss why this is important to those people. They should not be required to participate unless it is clear that, for younger children, their parents have knowingly given approval or, for older pupils, they have decided that they wish to do so.

It is particularly important that Anglican schools demonstrate sensitivity in this area if they have admitted pupils whose parents are members of other faiths.

Special Educational Needs

Pupils may have Special Educational Needs as a result of a variety of factors. A Church school will have a particular concern to ensure that their special needs, which are part of the child's uniqueness as a human being, meet with a suitable response.

Too often adults automatically use a deficit model when they consider pupils with special needs. In order to guard against such thinking, the first group of special needs that will be considered will be those resulting from particular abilities.

There will be some pupils in every school who have a particular academic, artistic, musical or sporting ability. How are such pupils challenged to achieve the most of which they are capable? While developing their talents how can a school ensure that they receive a rounded education?

There will be some pupils in every school who make normal or perhaps very good progress in most areas of school life, but find a particular concept or skill difficult to grasp and master. How does the school ensure that such pupils are helped and encouraged with the challenging aspects of their work? A moment's reflection will reveal that almost every pupil comes into this group from time to time.

There will be a few pupils in every school whose special needs are long term, some of them permanent. There are well-established procedures for identifying these needs and developing a strategy for meeting them within the context of the school. For those whose needs are greatest this will include developing a formal statement. Every school must have a teacher who is Special Educational Needs co-ordinator and a governor who takes particular responsibility for this area on behalf of the governors. For some of the pupils within the formal Special Educational Needs procedure, there are issues which are confidential. Governors not involved in Special Educational Needs work must accept that it may not be possible to share all the information about some pupils' needs.

In some schools there will be a need to ensure that buildings are adapted to improve the access for pupils or adults whose mobility is reduced. It is important that governors support such projects in order to ensure that they meet their responsibilities both for the children and for adults associated with the school.

In other schools the need may be for special equipment or special training for staff in order to ensure that the education of pupils is facilitated. In some cases finance or other resources will come from the LEA, Social Services or the Health Authority. Sometimes the school will meet these needs from its own budget.

For some pupils there is still a need for special education in units designed for their particularly severe needs. Many of these are based within mainstream schools and thus facilitate integration. A few of these units, probably for those pupils whose needs are so great that only such schools have the resources to provide for them, will be separate from mainstream schools.

There is one exercise that can help governors and managers review their approach to the full range of Special Educational Needs in their school. For each subject area or main activity within the school, ask three questions.

1. In this area of the school's life, how would pupils demonstrate that they had special abilities and how would we meet such pupils' needs?
2. In this area of the school's life, what short-term difficulties might pupils encounter and what action would be taken to help them?
3. In this area of the school's life, what specific long-term learning difficulties might pupils demonstrate and how would we help and sustain them through such problems?

Try this exercise for Mathematics, Music and Religious Education first. What does it tell you about your school?

School trips and journeys

At various times while they are at school, children should have the opportunity to take part in visits to places of interest as an integral part of the curriculum. They may also be offered the opportunity to participate in recreational activities as part of a school group. Both these types of activity are an important part of a child's overall educational experience. From the school's point of view they provide a broadening of the curriculum and an opportunity to know and understand the children more deeply as a result of seeing them in a different context and they make an important contribution to the social education programme in the school.

Every school trip, whether it is a walk to a local shop with nursery children or a field trip to a distant part of Europe with sixth formers, needs careful planning and preparation. There must also be good co-ordination with colleagues so that pupils are not faced with insoluble conflicts of interest or destructive competition between different departments' activities. The purpose, costs and timing of the trips will need to be carefully explained to parents so that they are in a position to make an informed judgement about their child's participation. Where a trip is an essential part of the curriculum, schools will need to establish how they are going to meet the costs, what part of these may be legitimately passed on to parents and how the children whose parents cannot afford such costs will be enabled to take part. Where the trip is desirable but not essential, and is therefore happening outside main school time, it will presumably be self-financing.

Governors will need to be satisfied that the school's arrangements for such trips take full account of the governors' responsibilities for the health and safety of their staff.

The variety of children in the care of the school

This chapter began with a statement about children. It is a true statement, but within it lies a great danger. Children are not a thing. Children are a collection of individuals. Every one is unique. A school can only be about children insofar as it is about each individual child.

It is common today to hear calls for the return to class teaching. This conjures up images of teachers standing in front of classes of children teaching them. There is nothing wrong with class teaching. It can be an effective means of enabling children to learn, but it does have some limitations.

Picture the scene in the classroom. The teacher is teaching the class. The teacher is active. Are the children active? What are they learning? If you can answer the first question in the affirmative and you can answer the second question positively, then you are picturing effective class teaching.

As the number of children who are not learning increases, so there must be doubts about whether the class teaching is being effective. The test is always the child and what s/he is learning from the experience. Some topics lend themselves better to individual learning programmes than to class or group teaching. A wise teacher uses a mixture of all the possible techniques during the course of a day, so that it is more likely that every child will have experienced some useful learning.

The paragraph above has focused on the classroom, but examples could be taken from every aspect of the school day. The school's first duty is to the child. Each one individually. Even when the parents and the teachers are discussing the latest fund-raising proposals, the purpose is still to make the school a better place for the children for whom they share a concern and commitment.

For more information

- Connect to the churchschools.co.uk web site.
- Put in your password to access the welcome menu.
- Follow the link to Church School Management.
- Select the **pupils** section using the button on the menu.

The **pupils** section will open onscreen. Here you will find the text of this chapter together with links to more detailed information.

- Follow the links to the subsections that you need.

http://www.churchschools.co.uk

There Are No Schools Without Parents

If the primary concern of schools is the individual child, then that quickly brings the school into a close relationship with the parents of that child. In this chapter parents will be used to cover a wide range of individuals and circumstances. Some children have only one parent living with them. Some will have several adults who care for them and are involved in their nurture and concerned for their future. 'Parents' covers, to a greater or lesser extent, all those adults whose concern is for the child. The school will see some of these parents regularly, others hardly at all. It is a great mistake to assume that an unseen parent is an uncaring parent.

Parents are the primary educators of children. Schools must work in partnership with parents wherever possible. Good partnerships start with good communication, mutual trust and respect. It is for schools to take the initiatives that create these conditions.

Schools must plan their relationships with parents carefully. Teachers and others, particularly office staff, who communicate regularly with parents all need to understand what type of relationships the school is trying to establish with parents and how they, as professionals, contribute to them. This chapter will consider a number of points of contact with parents, all of which are significant in the establishment of good relations between the school and the children's parents.

First contact: the school brochure

For many parents the first formal communication from the school will be the school brochure. There may have been informal contact with the head teacher or the school secretary in order to obtain it, and those conversations will have begun to set the tone for future relationships, but the first formal statements will be in the brochure. It is not surprising that many schools have put much effort into the production of these brochures. It is surprising that so many schools fail to check the legal requirements concerning them. There is a detailed list of the required contents of schools brochures, but very few schools seem to comply with the list completely. Governors need to ensure that those preparing or reviewing the school brochure have checked the legal requirements recently and ensured that they are all met.

The legal requirements are the minimum that the school brochure should contain. Governors should also establish what they wish to see in the brochure to help parents gain an accurate picture of the school. In particular, Church schools will wish to make the links between the school and the church community clear. Pictures may help to convey a good image; advertising or sponsorship may help pay for the costs of production but the key question must always be: 'How does this brochure help parents to understand the school and what it offers their child?' Some governors may feel that it is worthwhile asking someone outside the school community to check a draft of the text for them with this question in mind.

Home/school agreements

Every school must create a home/school agreement. The governors must consult with parents on the content of the agreement and a copy of it must be provided to every new parent when their child is first offered a place at the school. In primary schools where there is a pre-school meeting with parents, this may provide a good opportunity to explain the agreement. Schools must ensure that they deliver their side. This implies that every member of staff knows what is in the agreement and how it affects their approach to their work. Parents are not required to sign the agreement, nor can there be any attempt to make its terms binding on them. The agreement will lay out the school's expectations of parents and pupils as well as how the school will provide for the child's education in partnership with the parents. This should assist and promote good relations with parents, as it will avoid some of the misunderstandings that lead to breakdowns in relationships.

The basic agreements may also be helpful when situations arise that create cause for concern in the behaviour or attitude of a particular child. Re-negotiation of the agreement or a clarification of its principles may form part of the discussion with the child's parents, designed to develop a joint strategy between the parents and the school to achieve an improvement in the situation.

Communication

Communication between home and school is often a cause of difficulty and frustration. Many factors are involved. These include:

- the telephone manner of the staff in the school office, including the head teacher;
- the linguistic style used in letters home by individual teachers or by the school clerical staff;
- the differences between the language registers used by teachers and by parents;
- the style of leadership adopted by the head teacher, teachers or governors at meetings for parents;
- stress levels;
- the accuracy of the school-gate gossip.

Not all these factors are within the control of the school. Some are unconscious habits that may have to be studiously unlearned.

The school staff and governors, however, must take the initiative to improve communications. It is reasonable to hope that parents will respond to the school's best efforts with understanding and courtesy, but it cannot be guaranteed. This is not an excuse for the school to give up making the effort to communicate well. Governors who are prepared to meet with parents or other members of the community, to explain to them what the school is doing and why, have much to contribute to the school in the development of good communication. Governors who join the parents in pressurizing a school for change may not always be assisting the cause of good communication.

One final thought on communication. Teachers, even head teachers, do not often have cause to contact the school from outside during working hours. As a result, they may be unaware of the impression given to callers over the telephone. The governor who compliments the school secretary in the hearing of the head teacher on her manner with callers can make a major contribution to the re-enforcement of good practice in the school.

Annual report and meeting

The governing body of every school must prepare an annual report for its parents. The annual report must contain all the items required by law. These include details of the action plan following any inspection of the school and the latest test or examination results. The report is, however, the governors' account of their work for the year. This means that there are always likely to be items in the report which are not required by law, but which are important to the school.

It is important that the governors are active in the preparation of the report and its presentation to the parents. This presentation is given at the Annual Parents' Meeting. It is good practice for the chairs of governors' sub-committees to present the section of the report that relates to the work of their sub-committee. This not only makes the presentation more interesting, but also gives parents a feel for how the governors exercise their responsibilities.

Parents must be provided with written notice of the date of the Annual Parents' Meeting. It is for the governors to decide how they will define the word 'parent'. This can be important on those rare occasions when there can be a vote. In general terms these meetings are an opportunity for governors and staff to involve the parents in the life of the school and to answer any questions which parents may have. The meetings complement, but should not seek to duplicate, the regular meetings between class teachers and parents, when the progress of their child or children can be discussed. The subjects discussed at the meeting should be general ones. Discussion of individual teachers should never be allowed. Wherever possible it should be clear to parents that interesting and important issues will be discussed, so that as many parents as possible are encouraged to attend. It should not be assumed that low attendance indicates that all is well with the school.

Informal social work

For many head teachers, one aspect of the maintenance of good relationships with parents is both demanding of time and professionally challenging. There are many parents who, having confidence in the school, use the head teacher and sometimes other members of staff as a source of advice, help and good counsel. It is not clear why head teachers should be seen in this role, except that they are usually experienced adults who are readily contactable. It can be difficult to make an appointment with a doctor or a social worker. The head teacher is on the premises of the school for most of most days and has a concern for the welfare of the family. This derives from the knowledge that problems within the family setting have a potentially significant impact on the children's ability to profit from their schooling. Within certain limits, therefore, head teachers become involved in the worries and concerns of the family.

The first paragraph of this section has referred to the head teacher as the focus of the work. This is justified by the fact that in most primary schools the head teacher will be the member of staff most often involved, although other staff may also contribute. In secondary schools the pastoral staff will do much of the work of this nature. In some schools, the school secretary will fulfil the role for some parents. While acknowledging this, this section will, for brevity, continue to discuss the issues as if it is always the head teacher who undertakes the task.

What are the limits?

Ideally the head teacher should be in the position of a listener who can then point those who need it in the direction of appropriate sources of help. In Church schools this will include the parish priest.

Ideally the head teacher only becomes involved to the extent that it does not interfere with his/her duty to the children in the school's care.

Ideally the head teacher should not become so personally involved in the issues that it affects his or her work or home life.

The emphasis on 'ideally' in these statements is intended to acknowledge that the best of intentions do not signify much when a parent arrives at the school at five to nine in the morning announcing in a flood of tears that their partner has left the home, taking all the family money but none of the debts. Well-ordered schedules for the day's work are put aside in response to the human need of the moment. At the end of the day the head may be in need of someone with whom to talk through the experience. Good resolutions about not becoming involved will have been discarded.

What can be done?

The school needs to acknowledge that responding to incidents such as the one sketched out above is part of the school's task. Some thought can then be given to enabling this aspect of the work to be done as effectively as possible.

- The school should have, readily accessible, the contact names and telephone numbers for the local offices of the various agencies who offer expertise, guidance or support across a wide range of problems.
- Support for the head teacher should be well managed. Where possible, supplies of tea or coffee should be made available. The opportunity to complete the interview with the parent in privacy and uninterrupted should be facilitated by other members of staff, who can ensure that the telephone is answered quickly and that those wishing to speak to the head teacher on non-urgent topics are encouraged to find another time for the discussion.
- All members of staff should observe absolute confidentiality on these incidents.
- The head teacher should have someone who can provide a debriefing service if this is needed. There is nothing sophisticated about this. What is needed is a good listener who is not involved in the school or the immediate community and is prepared to listen while the head teacher talks through what has happened and his/her response to it.

None of these measures solve the problems, but they may help to keep them in perspective. One final point may also help. If governors and colleagues know that this work is done, they should be able to offer support and appreciation without having to be told any details that would breach the trust that the parents have placed in the school.

Parent/Teacher Associations

Every school will have an organization that brings together parents, teachers and sometimes the supporters of the school from the wider community. The organization may be fairly formally structured or it may operate very informally. What is right for one type of community at one point in time may not be right for the same community ten years later or the next-door community now. The prime tasks of such an organization will include:

- support for the school, including, but not exclusively, fund-raising;
- enhanced communication and partnership between staff, parents and the wider community;
- social and educational activities for parents and families associated with the school.

Many other things may also happen, but these seem to be at the heart of such organizations.

Parent/teacher organizations are, like most other human organizations, subject to the strengths and weaknesses of the human beings who make up the membership.

Parent/Teacher Associations or similar organizations will need to have an established formal structure if they are to raise funds. There are model PTA constitutions available. Whatever structure is adopted, it should make clear:

- how the committee is elected;
- how the committee's membership will be regularly renewed;
- how the purposes of the organization are defined;
- how it will organize its financial affairs;
- how the organization can be wound up;

- how the organization will relate to the governors and, in a Church school, to the Church.

The problem with parents

One of the problems facing anyone trying to write about parents is the plural. There are no such things as parents. There are individuals made in God's image, who are attempting to bring up their children to the best of their ability. In contrast to the school's stance towards pupils, which will be impartial, every parent will be partial for his or her children; that is, they will take their children's part. It is no good expecting parents to be impartial, to understand both sides; they want the best for their children. They expect the school to provide this, particularly if they have chosen the school themselves rather than leaving the choice to chance – the school with a vacancy or the nearest to their house.

Teachers and other members of the staff of the school need to build up an atmosphere of trust, collaboration and partnership between themselves and parents. Where this is created there is a reasonable prospect of harmonious working together in the interests of the child, at least some of the time.

Parents are not always correct in their judgements, of course, nor do they always nourish realistic dreams of what their child will achieve in school or in the world beyond. Sometimes schools will need to protect children from the pressures that parents put on them. Occasionally teachers may need to sustain the child's dream in the face of parental opposition. Rarely, teachers may have to help to protect a child from the physical or mental abuse that is offered by a few parents. Parents are not always right, they do not always know best. Teachers are not always right either, they do not always know best. The same may also be said for governors and for all other human beings. In the main, all of us try to do our best and sometimes we may even succeed. Many children will succeed despite our failures, perhaps as many as will succeed as a result of our successes.

The rights and responsibilities of parents

Parents do have rights within education law and it is important that the school honours these. Some of these rights affect the curriculum; others are concerned with their relationship with the school, the teachers and the governors. Details of parental rights are provided on the web site. Listed in detail, these rights can sound formidable. They are there, however, to safeguard the parents' position and to ensure that they receive all the information about their child's education that they should reasonably expect. To balance these rights, parents also have responsibilities. The responsibilities include:

- ensuring that their child attends the school regularly and on time;
- collaborating with the school to ensure that their child obeys reasonable school rules and completes tasks set for homework;
- collaborating with the school on measures for the security of all pupils and staff.

The key principle within all these rights and responsibilities is that in any good school there must be a well-developed partnership between the staff of the school and the parents. Without such a partnership very little that is positive can be achieved.

Representation

There are two distinct issues contained within this section. One is how parents can make representations to the school over issues that affect only their children or a small number of others. The second is how parents can make their views known on general issues of school policy and organization.

In the first instance, there needs to be a well-established pattern of meetings with teachers and appropriate levels of school management to ensure that there are good, open relationships and that if an issue arises it can, whenever possible, be dealt with speedily and effectively. A key point in such a process will be the opportunity that parents have to meet and discuss the issue with the head teacher. Regardless of the size of the school and the accessibility of the head teacher, the meeting between the parents and the head teacher has formal significance. If the issue cannot be resolved at such a meeting, the options that are open to parents to take the matter further inevitably generate formal action and processes. Parents have the right to take a complaint forward to the governing body if they are not satisfied with the response they have received from the head teacher.

On the more general issues of parents being represented within the formal structures for the governance and management of the school, they are represented on the school governing body through their elected representatives and, in Voluntary Aided schools, by those foundation governors who must also be parents. It is important that the school ensures that all parents are kept informed of the names of their representatives so that they can make their views known to them.

A further form of representation will be through the Parent/Teacher Association or its equivalent in the school.

Home–school transport

The issues that arise around the journey to and from school are quite complex. They derive from the concern to ensure that all pupils are provided with a safe and appropriate arrangement to get them to and from school. In 1944 certain assumptions were made about the distances that children of different ages could travel safely. These have been clarified by subsequent judgements in the courts. Over the years, public perception of what is appropriate and safe has changed but the legal definitions have not.

For Church schools the issue also involves the extent to which the appropriate school for the child may be a Church school, even when this is not the nearest school.

For Local Education Authorities the issues of cost are also important. The provision of coaches and taxis every day to ensure that all pupils arrive at school on time and are delivered safely home at the end of the school day creates a complex administrative task with a significant cost element. This is particularly important for those pupils who have to be transported to special schools, where specially adapted vehicles and trained escorts may have to be provided.

Local Education Authorities must provide free transport to school for those pupils under eight who live more than two miles from their nearest appropriate school and for those over that age who live more than three miles from their nearest appropriate school. Local Education Authorities may choose to provide transport to the nearest Church school, where this is beyond the travel limits for children, when the parents adhere to the faith or denomination to which the school is affiliated. Most Local Education Authorities have done this for many years. In setting their admissions policies, governors will need to be aware of the Local Education Authority's policy on this issue in order to avoid setting up expectations among parents that will not be met.

Several government initiatives have been pursued in recent years on the issue of home to school transport, aimed at reducing the traffic congestion caused in many areas by the 'school run' and also the perceived growth of car dependency amongst children. These initiatives have usually focused on the creation of safer walking and cycling routes to and from school.

For more information

- Connect to the churchschools.co.uk web site.
- Put in your password to access the welcome menu.
- Follow the link to Church School Management.
- Select the **parents** section using the button on the menu.

The **parents** section will open onscreen. Here you will find the text of this chapter together with links to more detailed information.

- Follow the links to the subsections that you need.

http://www.churchschools.co.uk

Staff: The Most Important Resource in the School

The staff of a Church school are its most important asset. Next to the pupils they are the most important people in the school. Through them the educational objectives of the school are delivered. They share with the governors of the school the task of preserving the school's identity within the Anglican tradition of education. Many of the staff will be professionally trained and experienced. Some will be employed entirely because their personal qualities are appropriate to one of the many tasks that the school must fulfil. All must be aware of their role within the overall policy and ethos of the school. All will require induction into the school traditions. All will require training, support, management, direction and opportunities for further development. This chapter will consider the principles underlying the employment of support staff, contract staff, teachers and senior managers within the school. They apply to all categories of school.

Employment

Support staff

Within this general category fall all those staff of the school who are not teachers. Some of these staff will be employed on an hourly or part-time basis. Some will be full-time employees. Some will need specific qualifications and experience to undertake their responsibilities. Some will simply need a willingness to undertake the task and the personal qualities appropriate to it. Without them the school could not function.

In Voluntary Aided and Foundation schools the governors are the employers of all the staff within this category except kitchen staff and those employed by contractors. While governors may develop their own policies with regard to their staff, they must work within the framework of employment law. This means, in particular, that they are not able to discriminate on the employment of these members of staff on religious grounds. Staff should know that they must act in accordance with school policies, provided that these policies are not themselves a form of hidden discrimination. The National Society has prepared forms of contract for staff in these categories. Governors need to be satisfied that those responsible for administering these contracts are completing them in accordance with the guidance provided by the Society. This is particularly important for part-time staff and those who will only be working during term time.

In Voluntary Controlled schools the LEA is the employer, but many of the employment functions will be delegated to the school. Governors must act within the policies laid down by the LEA in the appointment of support staff and should seek the advice of the appropriate department if they are in doubt. They must not act in ways which exceed their delegated powers under Local Management of Schools (LMS).

Staff employed by others to carry out work in the school on contract

The essence of this group of staff, which may include cleaners, kitchen staff and ground maintenance workers as well as employees of builders, is that they are not employed by the governing body or the LEA. Before any contract is awarded to a contractor it is important that the governors, the school managers and the contractors have a clear understanding of how the staff undertaking the work will conduct themselves. If they are to have unsupervised access to children, the contractor must be able to provide evidence that the appropriate police checks have been carried out.

Should there be concerns about such staff in terms of either their performance or their conduct towards pupils or other staff, these issues will need to be dealt with in accordance with previously agreed procedures. It is essential that school managers or governors do not interfere with the established patterns of management. This can lead to confusion and, in some cases, increased costs. It is also important to ensure that those employees of contractors who are engaged in work which can affect the general ethos of the school are appropriately trained to understand their role. Great care needs to be taken in this area by Church schools. The head teacher should be prepared to work with the manager of the contractor's staff to ensure that everyone understands what is required of them. The most obvious example of staff in this category are those involved in making, serving or supervising school meals.

This group of employees may be working in schools of any category. The issues are basically the same for all.

Teachers

In Voluntary Aided and Foundation schools the teachers are employees of the governing body. The LEA provides the finance through the delegated budget and in most schools may provide payroll services. It has been traditional in Voluntary Aided schools to refer to the division of responsibilities between governors and LEA as that between employer and paymaster. This is still useful but may, in future years, break down if a significant number of governing bodies decide to cease to use LEA payroll facilities.

In Voluntary Aided schools governors may decide to discriminate in the appointment of teachers in favour of candidates who can demonstrate a positive commitment to the faith of the school. Governors need to decide how they will use this right in any particular appointment to the school's teaching staff. They should make their intentions clear in both their advertisements and their job or person specification. This is a special right available to the governors of Voluntary Aided schools and is not affected by current human rights legislation.

In Foundation schools the governors cannot discriminate in teacher appointments in the way that Voluntary Aided schools can. Only in the specific area of the appointment of reserved teachers may they explore the candidate's suitability to teach Religious Education in accordance with the teachings of the faith or denomination of the school. Reserved teachers are a special feature of Foundation and Voluntary Controlled schools that have a religious foundation. Their existence is based on the rights of parents to choose to have Religious Education taught in accordance with a church rather than a LEA syllabus (see page 83). Reserved teachers are those who could teach RE in accordance with a church syllabus if the parents ask for it. Governors will need to have a clear understanding of how RE for a Church school is currently given particular expression in their school, in order to be able to assess the suitability of a candidate for a post which carries the responsibility of a reserved teacher.

In Voluntary Controlled schools the teachers are the employees of the LEA, although many of the functions of employer are delegated to the governing body. In all teacher posts except reserved teachers, the governors must follow the employment policies of the local authority. The comments on reserved teachers in the paragraph on Foundation schools also apply to Voluntary Controlled schools.

Where schools with a religious character have established an ethos statement, this should form part of the information sent to all candidates for teaching posts. They can be expected to support the ethos of the school where they have chosen to teach. This applies to all categories of school.

Head teachers

The head teacher is the key appointment in any school. All studies of successful schools identify the role played in the school by the head teacher as being critical. It has been suggested that the most important contribution that governors can make to their school is to appoint the right head teacher.

In Voluntary Aided schools the head teacher is an employee of the governors. Normally the governors will be looking to appoint a very successful teacher with a clear understanding of school management and a strong commitment to the Anglican Church. Sometimes a candidate who is actively involved in another Christian denomination will be the best candidate, but it is difficult to see how someone without a strong Christian commitment can provide the Christian leadership necessary for the school to be a good Church school.

Every candidate for the post of head teacher should be able to demonstrate that they have made a thorough professional preparation for the post. This will include completion of the National Professional Qualification for Head teachers, but on its own this will only rarely be sufficient. Good candidates will have taken advantage of one of the opportunities provided by dioceses, Church Colleges or the National Society to study the specific issues which distinguish Church schools from Community schools.

In Foundation and Voluntary Controlled schools slightly different issues arise. Governors, whether they are the employers (Foundation schools) or working under delegation from the LEA, cannot discriminate on faith grounds in the same way that the governors of Voluntary Aided schools can. They must work within the framework of equal opportunities and human rights legislation that applies to Community schools. There is one important proviso, however. In both Foundation and Voluntary Controlled schools the governors have the explicit right under the School Standards and Framework Act to assure themselves that any candidate for the headship of their school is able to sustain and develop the ethos of the school. Candidates will demonstrate this ability both by evidence of professional preparation and by their answers to the questions that the governors ask about the professional issues involved in managing an Anglican school. It will be important for governors to distinguish carefully between asking candidates about their personal beliefs and asking them about their professional attitudes. It is the latter which should be explored with every candidate.

The appointing process for all staff

Before a governing body proceeds to make any appointment, they must ensure that all the basic steps required by good appointing practice have been taken: These are detailed on the web site; in summary they include:

1. selecting those who will be making the appointment;
2. ensuring that those making the appointment have been given the authority to do so;
3. contacting those persons who have a right to attend for the purpose of giving advice and involve them in the planning;
4. drawing up a job description, or check that the existing one still applies;
5. drawing up a person specification, or check that the existing one still applies;
6. checking that the application form will elicit the information needed;

7. ensuring that the budget can cover the costs of the appointment;
8. establishing a timetable for the appointing process;
9. advertising or otherwise making the existence of the post known;
10. drawing up a short list of those candidates who most nearly match the job and person specification;
11. arranging for these candidates to visit the school and ask questions about the nature of the post;
12. ensuring that the interviewers can be present at the whole of the interviewing and decision-making process.

Each of these steps could be further broken down into sub-steps. Some may appear to be so standard or routine that they are obvious. Each needs to be completed. The National Society can provide examples of incidents where failure to complete each of these steps has led to subsequent problems or challenges.

Once all these steps have been completed, the school will be in a position to conduct the part of the selection process in which the most appropriate candidate is finally selected. The interviews should be conducted by members of the governing body or by senior managers within the school who have been delegated the necessary powers.

During the interview every candidate should be asked the same basic questions. The questions should relate to the job and person specification prepared by the governors. The governors should ensure that, if they do not possess the specialist knowledge necessary to frame appropriate technical questions and evaluate the answers, they have an adviser or specialist with them to assist with the interview process.

Governors should ensure that notes are kept of each interview – preferably by more than one of the interviewers. Sometimes it is helpful to provide prepared forms for note-taking which help interviewers to relate what is being said to the requirements of the post.

When the interviews are complete the interviewers should proceed to evaluate the candidates' suitability and potential. Steps should be taken to ensure that those who are making judgements do so carefully and make full use of the criteria that have been established for the post. It is unfair to all the candidates if any of those making the decisions use information other than that contained in the application and the formal references or elicited during the interview. If any of the candidates are known personally to the governors, this knowledge should be declared and conscious efforts made to ensure that it does not influence the decision.

Someone from the interviewing panel, usually a person with specialist knowledge of the post, should be prepared to offer unsuccessful candidates comments on their performance during the interview. This can require skill and tact. The 'feedback' process is intended to help unsuccessful candidates to learn constructively from the experience.

Governors must agree with a successful candidate for the headship of the school the points on the salary scale that will be used to establish the remuneration. All those involved in these negotiations on behalf of the governors should be aware of the school pay policy and the budgetary and personnel implications of any departure from the agreed policy. The clearer that the governors can be on this issue when the post is advertised, the easier the subsequent discussions are likely to be. Governors must avoid being trapped into discussing the remuneration package from scratch after the post has been offered and accepted.

Development

Induction

The first few days in a new post can be challenging and confusing even for an experienced professional. It is very important that there are good arrangements for the induction of any new employee. This applies whether the employee is the head teacher or the cleaner. The principles are the same. Anyone joining the staff needs to learn about the layout of the buildings, key school policies that will affect them and their work, the overall management structure of the school and how they personally will fit into to it. They will need to meet key colleagues. They will need to feel that they are welcomed into the school and that people are committed to supporting them in their work. For many posts it will be appropriate to ask someone to act as a mentor for the first few weeks or months to ensure that the new employee has continuing support and makes the best possible start in their new post. For head teachers a mentor may be a serving head teacher from another similar school within a reasonable distance.

Being a mentor is a major professional responsibility. Good mentoring can help new employees feel part of the team quickly. It can help them reach an effective level of professional performance as soon as possible. Poor mentoring can lead to disillusionment and alienation. Good mentors are able to provide support, information and encouragement in equal proportions. They also provide guidance on the way in which the school or the authority is organized and how an individual can extract the best from the institution and work at their best within it. There are no quick guides for mentors on how they are able to achieve this. Essentially, they have to develop their role as an interaction with the individual they are mentoring.

For teachers in their first year of teaching after qualification, special arrangements apply. These are laid out in guidance from the appropriate government agency. Those responsible for appointing such teachers must be certain that the proper arrangements have been made to ensure that the newly qualified teacher makes the best possible start in his or her chosen profession.

Continuing support

Even when the individual has been successfully inducted into their new post, the need for support in it does not end. Staff will need continuing opportunities to develop their skills. This implies that training must be an ongoing process throughout a person's service in the school. Involvement in a continuing programme of training is important for the individual's professional development and for the school's continuing improvement. Some of the training may derive from the school performance management process. All will relate to the school's Educational Development Plan (Education Strategic Plan in Wales).

Training is as important for support staff as it is for teachers, so there will be no one in the school whose training needs are neglected. Governors should be aware of developments in training opportunities open to teachers. The Teacher Training Agency has developed a range of training schemes appropriate to the stages in a teacher's career. These stages include induction, subject leadership, preparation for headship and programmes for newly appointed and experienced head teachers. Teachers preparing for, or at, these stages in their careers should be encouraged to take part in these schemes. The Church Colleges, working with the National Society, have developed award-bearing courses specifically related to the needs of teachers working in Church schools. These courses can be followed either by attendance at lectures or through distance learning. The colleges have also developed a certificated programme of training for governors.

Support for staff goes beyond the provision of training, however. It includes good management, both from the senior managers in the school and from any other colleagues who have line manager responsibilities. Governors also contribute to the management of the school by their interest and by the policies which they approve or develop. There will be governors who have a direct involvement in staff management through their role on the school staffing sub-committee. They will need to ensure that they act in concert with the paid managers of the school, so that employees perceive their managers to be operating consistently and fairly.

One aspect of good management is concern for the long-term career development of staff. Promotion, internal or external, will be a key aspect of career development, as will training, study and skill development. Governors have a key role to play in these issues, as they will often be called upon to make decisions that affect the careers of the staff of the school. It is helpful if governors occasionally refresh their understanding of the patterns of career development open to staff in their school. Some career moves need careful preparation; some involve an element of risk taking. It is the task of the senior management of the school to provide guidance and encouragement to individual employees within the context of the school programme of performance management. Governors need to support this process. Sometimes, particularly in primary schools, the next move in the career and professional development of a teacher will involve a change of school. It is helpful if governors recognize that this is the case and do not seek to discourage teachers from a commitment to their own careers, even if this means that the teacher leaves their schools.

An important aspect of good staff management will be the establishment of an appropriate, fair and affordable pay policy. Governors have limited discretion on the salary and benefits that can be provided for their staff. The policy must stay within the limits that are set by law and by the LEA Fair Funding Scheme.

Another aspect of support for staff is the conditions in which they are required to work and the extent to which the school buildings represent a good environment. Governors should be aware of the adequacy of the staff facilities. For example:

- Is the staff room large enough to accommodate all the adults who may need to meet for their breaks or for a staff meeting?
- Are the facilities in which the staff work in good condition and well cared for?
- Do those staff who need space to interview people in private have access to appropriate rooms?
- Do those staff who need to store specialist equipment or to change for specialist activities have the facilities that they need? Are they adequate for their purpose and well maintained?

Much publicity has been given in recent years to the need for schools to ensure that their security systems are adequate. Staff need to know that they can work in an environment where they are as secure as possible from the threat of attack, and that they can summon help quickly should they feel threatened. The measures that the governors need to take in any particular school will depend on a careful risk assessment exercise on their school, taking account of advice from the Health and Safety Executive and the Department for Education and Employment/Welsh Assembly. If there is a local school watch scheme, governors should consider ensuring that their school is a fully participating member of the scheme.

Sometimes there will be circumstances, perhaps within the personal life of a colleague, when an individual member of staff needs a significant level of support and understanding in order to help them through a crisis. Senior managers will need to act with sensitivity and flexibility in such circumstances. A failure to handle one incident of this nature appropriately will quickly have an impact on a whole range of staff attitudes. 'They wouldn't even let me have time off to go to my mother's funeral', if true, can undermine years of work to generate a family atmosphere within a school.

Appraisal

An important part of any system of staff support is appraisal. Regular meetings to review progress and needs with a senior manager should help staff to maintain a proper view of their performance and value as a professional. This is not just an issue for teaching staff.

There is a national framework for teacher appraisal set in the context of performance management from which LEAs have developed their own schemes. LEA schemes should include appropriate provisions for Church schools. Governors need to be clear about the way in which appraisal operates within their school. They need to be satisfied that all staff have had appropriate training in the appraisal system in use in the school. Governors also need to ensure that the process is properly supported by an allocation of funds to ensure that any identified training need can be met. This is a key factor in a satisfactory appraisal process. If the result of an appraisal process is the identification of a training need that is not subsequently met, all that has been achieved is the de-skilling of the person being appraised.

The appraisal of head teachers is of particular importance for two reasons. First, it sets the tone and standard for the appraisals of the rest of the staff. Secondly, it is more complex because it will involve external appraisers. In a Church school at least one of these external appraisers should have personal experience of work in a similar school. For many members of staff the Church school ethos and their contribution to it will be an important aspect of the appraisal process.

One of the governors, who has been nominated for this purpose by the governing body, will receive reports on the appraisal process from the head teacher. These reports are provided to the governors so that they may be sure that the appraisal process is being monitored effectively. It will also ensure that there is a governor who can speak on the issue of staff training and development needs when the governors are discussing the school budget.

Other governors may be asked to provide evidence to the appraiser, when their responsibilities mean that they work closely with the head teacher or other teacher who is being appraised.

The National Society and a number of dioceses have taken steps to ensure that there are publications and training opportunities for teachers and other staff working in Church schools, which can be used as part of a planned follow-up to appraisal.

Discipline, grievances and competence

In this short introduction to the many issues that arise when one of these procedures is likely to be used, the focus will be on general principles. Should any senior manager or governor feel that a difficult situation is likely to develop in their school, they should immediately seek the advice of their Diocesan Director of Education, certainly before any decisions are taken. Too often difficult situations have been made worse by people trying to act without first taking advice.

All staff should have signed a contract that contains a procedure to be used in cases where discipline, grievance or competence issues arise. One of the important aspects of this contract is that it should accurately reflect the employment arrangements in the school. The key issue is who will hear any appeal. The legal employers must hear it. If the governors are the employers (Voluntary Aided and Foundation) then any formal procedures must reflect this. If the LEA is the employer (Voluntary Controlled) then the LEA will arrange a committee to hear the appeal. In an Anglican school there will be a significant tension for the governors and senior staff of the school in the rare instances when these issues arise. They will wish to ensure that all staff maintain the highest standards, but they will also be concerned that the pastoral needs of all those involved in the situation are responded to appropriately. It is not normally possible for the same person to be both active in the hearings and providing pastoral care for one of the other parties. Governors will want to be satisfied that arrangements have been put in hand for the pastoral support of all individuals, while they deal with those areas of the situation which are their responsibility as employers. Diocesan Directors of Education should be asked to provide advice and guidance on all matters to do with these hearings. They can be particularly supportive in assisting the governing body to work through the tensions between the need for formal proceedings and the pastoral care of all the individuals involved in the process.

One of the most difficult problems facing governors and senior managers in any of these situations is that of being able to demonstrate that they have been fair to all parties. If they have discussed the issues before any hearing, they could be perceived as having prejudiced their judgement. It is hard for governors who are concerned for and involved in their school to accept guidance that says 'You should not discuss this issue at this time, as there could be a formal hearing related to it at some point in the future'. It is, however, essential that they do accept such advice, if it is given.

It is also important that after a hearing those involved in it do not discuss the result or the content with their colleagues on the governing body. There may have to be an appeal and, therefore, a need for governors to be available who have not yet heard the arguments on either side.

Once an issue has been decided by the due process, it is essential that all parties stick closely to any agreements that have been made. It is usually helpful for there to be an agreement about what, if anything, will be said to staff, parents, press or the general enquirer. No one in the governing body or the schools management should deviate from such an agreement. This can be particularly important if there is significant local or press interest in the issue.

Staff absence

Members of staff may be absent from the school for a number of reasons. These will include attendance at meetings and courses as well as absence related to health issues. For the person responsible for ensuring that every class has a teacher, any absence is inconvenient. For teachers asked to cover for absent colleagues, any absence is costly in terms of time that has been committed to other activities. It is very important that absence is monitored and appropriate steps taken to reduce the impact of absence to a minimum.

Five different types of absence related to health issues may be identified. They each call for a different response and all present challenges to school management.

1. *Normal sickness*, that is, short periods of absence resulting from infections, accidents or other cause within the hazards of every day life. Except during periods of epidemic, schools normally cope with these occurrences, if not with ease, at least with efficiency. One problem faced by many schools is that many staff, knowing the potential disruption caused by any absence, come to work when they should have remained at home. This can delay their return to full fitness.

2. *Repeated absenteeism*, that is, when a member of staff has a series of short periods of absence, beyond that which can be put down to 'normal sickness'. Staff absence needs to be carefully monitored so that absenteeism can be identified and appropriate action taken. It may be that such absence is a symptom of excess stress or anxiety. Action to reduce the stress being experienced by the member of staff may improve attendance.
3. *Maternity/paternity leave*. There is a legal framework for such leave, and schools should seek to ensure that they comply suitably with the law, and with some flexibility, to meet the particular needs of staff members.
4. *Long-term sickness* resulting from a medical condition which, once diagnosed and treated, should result in a full recovery being made. These issues will arise from time to time in every school. It is clearly helpful to the school if the member of staff can ensure that the school is informed of the likely length of absence needed to complete the recovery. This information will need to be reviewed from time to time.
5. *Chronic illness* resulting from a permanent condition. There are many teachers who work very effectively while suffering from such conditions. Occasionally they may need a short time away from work for treatment or because the condition has temporarily become worse. Some chronic conditions deteriorate over time. In such cases, where it becomes clear that it is no longer possible for them to continue to work, it may be possible for them to receive a breakdown pension. In such circumstances the school will need to act supportively and with great sensitivity.

All of the above comments assume that the absences are brought on by the chances of life. A tiny minority of teachers choose a lifestyle that leads to absences from school which call forth less sympathy or understanding. Stereotypically, those who abuse alcohol would probably fall into this category. Management will need to act positively to ensure that such teachers do not become a burden on the school. Advice on these issues should always be sought before action is taken in individual cases.

Leaving and retirement

Schools are not just responsible for staff while they are employed at the school. They should be concerned and interested in them after they leave. Two examples will serve to illustrate the point.

- Do you remember Mrs Smith who used to work here? Well, she is a head teacher now!' A teacher with great professional promise begins her career at the school. After a few good years' work within the school she is promoted to a new post in another school. All those involved with the induction and professional formation of this teacher should take satisfaction not only from her first promotion but also from her subsequent career. It reflects credit on the school.
- 'I look back on my spell in that school as time well spent.' When an employee retires, it is important that he can be sure that his work has been valued. The much-mocked retirement party and leaving present are actually an important part of this process. It may also be important for a senior manager or governor to attempt to put the individual's career in an appropriate, positive context. Individuals who have given many years to work deserve to be assured that this has been of value and importance, even if there have been differences of view or emphasis.

Students

Many schools will have a regular arrangement whereby students spend time in the school as part of their course. This may include school students on work experience and nursery nurse students and teachers on their period of initial training. Proper arrangements need to be in place to ensure that all those coming into the school as students are inducted into the school's pattern of work and expectations. Equally, care needs to be taken to ensure that their needs are properly catered for so that their time in school is a good experience. The induction of students will need to include an introduction to the school's policies that will affect them. These will include policies about the care of pupils, health and safety issues and confidentiality. If there is likely to be an issue of police clearance for child protection purposes, the school should satisfy itself that such clearances have been obtained by the placing institution. If there is any doubt on this matter the school should insist on taking the appropriate action itself to obtain the necessary clearance.

Volunteers

Many of the comments made about students will also apply to volunteers. Most, but not all,volunteers in the school are likely to be parents. For most volunteers the school will need to ensure that it has initiated the appropriate police clearance checks. There will need to be a period of induction into the school for all volunteers, although for many parents this may be quite short and informal. If the volunteer is undertaking work for which they have no recent training, the issue of the provision of training for the task may arise. It is usually helpful to discuss with the volunteer the boundaries for their work, both in terms of what they will and will not do in the school and in terms of the period for which they will do it. If it has been clear from the start that the volunteer has agreed to offer two hours a week for a term, then towards the end of that term they can either be thanked for their contribution or a new agreement can be discussed for the following term. Some volunteers give many years of service to a school; others use volunteering at school as a way of re-entering the labour market after a period of caring for their children. Schools gain much benefit from both kinds of volunteer.

This chapter can only provide an introduction to the complex issues involved in the staffing of schools. It is a most important subject and no one should feel inhibited from seeking advice on it from specialists in the diocese or LEA office.

Detailed guidance on all aspects of staff employment is available in a series of publications which have been developed as a joint project with the dioceses of London, Southwark and Oxford. The text of the forms and the publications themselves are available on the National Society web site.

For more information

- Connect to the churchschools.co.uk web site.
- Put in your password to access the welcome menu.
- Follow the link to Church School Management.
- Select the **staffing** section using the button on the menu.

The **staffing** section will open onscreen. Here you will find the text of this chapter together with links to more detailed information.

- Follow the links to the subsections that you need.

http://www.churchschools.co.uk

Governors: A Major Responsibility

In the last twenty years there has been a huge growth in the role and importance of school governors. Being a governor no longer involves turning up to one meeting a term and occasionally for worship at harvest or Christmas. It is now a major piece of Christian and community service. No one should undertake the role lightly. It involves time, energy and a willingness to become involved in the life of the school on a regular basis over a significant period of time. Churches should recognize and support all those who undertake the responsibility of being a governor in a Church school.

Membership of governing bodies

There are several types of governor in Church schools. The exact constitution of the governing body is laid down in the Instrument of Government and must comply with the legal requirements for the type and size of school.

Foundation governors

In Church schools this is the description of the church governors. In an Anglican school it is usual for the incumbent of the parish to be a member of the governing body because s/he is the incumbent. This is called being an *ex officio* governor. In rare cases the incumbent may not be able to be a governor. If this is the case s/he should contact the Diocesan Education Office, which will arrange for the Archdeacon to nominate someone else from the church to take on the duties. This is usually what happens if there is an interregnum. Other foundation governors will be members of the church. The Instrument of Government will indicate which church organization has the responsibility for nominating the foundation governors. In Anglican schools it is common for there to be a mixture of nominating bodies including the local Parochial Church Council and the Diocesan Board of Education. Some of the foundation governors must also be parents of pupils at the school at the time when they are nominated. It is helpful if the Instrument makes it clear who is responsible for ensuring that their nominees are parents.

Teacher governors

In every school there are arrangements for the teachers employed at the school to elect one or more of their number to the governing body. If a teacher governor moves to a post in another school they cease to be a governor and a new election is necessary.

The head teacher as a governor

The head teacher of the school may choose to be a member of the governing body. Although when this option first became a possibility many head teachers decided not to become governors, opinion has changed and a recent survey suggested that only 15 per cent of head teachers were not full members of the governing body of their school. The head teacher can change his or her mind about this decision at any time. If the head teacher decides not to be a member of the governing body s/he is still entitled to attend meetings of the governing body. If the head teacher is not a full member s/he cannot vote.

Parent governors

The parents of the school are entitled to vote for one or more of their number to serve as governors of the school. Any parent who is elected must have a child attending the school when s/he takes up office. If the child subsequently leaves, the parent may complete their full term of office but may not stand for re-election. It is for the governors to decide who is entitled to vote in an election for parent governor, although advice may be available from the LEA.

Parent governors from all schools in the LEA can elect one of their number to represent parents on the Education Committee of the Local Authority.

Local Education Authority governor

The LEA nominates one or more governors to the school. These may be councillors or people active in the local community. It may take a significant time for a new governor to be nominated by an LEA because the nomination usually requires committee approval. For this reason it is important that the clerk to the governing body acts quickly to notify the LEA when a vacancy for an LEA governor occurs. Such action reduces the time that the governing body has to operate without one of its members.

Minor Local Authority governor

In some schools, in areas where there is a local council which is different from the Local Education Authority, the local council (referred to as the Minor Local Authority) is entitled to nominate a governor for co-option. In rural areas the MLA governor can be an important link between the school and the local civil parish, community or town.

Co-opted governors

Some schools have provision within their Instrument of Government for the governing body to co-opt governors, often representing local industry, to full membership of the governing body. Such co-options are often related to partnerships that have developed between the school and local businesses.

The governors' responsibilities

All members of the governing body have similar responsibilities:

- They are responsible for the overall policies of the school and for ensuring that the head teacher manages the school in accordance with those policies.
- They are responsible for representing the interests of the group that elects or nominates them on the governing body. The foundation governors are therefore particularly responsible for ensuring that a Church school is organized in accordance with the traditions and practices of the Church.
- They are responsible for ensuring that the needs of the school are represented appropriately to the body that nominated or elected them.

It will be clear from the tasks listed above that much of the work of a governor is about communication.

The governors also have a duty to elect a chair each year, to conduct their business efficiently and fairly and to ensure that any funds entrusted to them are administered properly.

The chair of the governing body

Each year the governors must elect one of their number to chair their meetings. There is a tradition in Church schools that this is the incumbent. Most Church school governing bodies now attempt to find the most appropriate person to chair their meetings, usually one of the foundation governors. This may have the effect of freeing the incumbent to undertake more 'chaplaincy' duties in the school. The chair of the governors must be able to lead the work of the governing body and to take public responsibility for that work on occasions such as the annual meeting for parents.

Observers

Sometimes individuals may be invited to attend meetings of the governing body as observers. Such people may speak if invited to do so by the chair, but they may not vote. They must agree to be bound by the same rules of confidentiality and corporate responsibility as full members of the governing body.

The clerk to the governing body

The clerk to the governing body acts as secretary to the governors. S/he prepares the agenda (working with the chair and the head teacher), sends out notice of the meetings and takes the minutes. In some areas the LEA provides clerks as a service to the school. In other areas the governors have to find their own. It may not be advisable for a member of the staff of the school to be the clerk, as this could lead to a conflict of interest or to some embarrassment among colleagues. Occasionally a member of the governing body has undertaken the duties of clerk, but in recent years the practice of having a paid clerk has grown and it is anticipated that in future governors will be prevented from taking this post. The clerk may also receive and deal with correspondence on behalf of the governing body, although it is still not uncommon to find that a governor acts as correspondent.

The Chief Education Officer and the Diocesan Director of Education

The holders of both these offices, and their representatives, may attend the meetings of the governing body under certain circumstances. The reason for this is to enable the governors to draw on the advice available from these two offices. Governors should ensure that they have taken the necessary steps to enable them to benefit from such advice. If these two office holders have been given formal rights to attend to give advice, it is important that the clerk ensures that they receive proper notice of all the meetings, a copy of the agenda, the minutes and any other papers that are being presented at the meeting.

Committees

The governing body may appoint committees to undertake some of its work, although there are certain decisions that cannot be delegated. Two obvious examples of committees are the group that makes decisions about which children to admit to the school in Voluntary Aided or Foundation schools and the staffing committee. Some of the committees will meet regularly and form a permanent part of the work of the governors. Others will take the nature of informal working parties set up to undertake a particular task and ending their work when that task is complete. It is important that the governing body gives any group that it creates a clear brief, so that there are no misunderstandings. It is also important that everyone knows whether the committee has decision-making powers or not. The full governing body should not re-debate issues that it has delegated to committees, unless the committee requests further guidance on policy issues. It is not necessary for every member of a committee to be a full member of the governing body.

Duties of governors

The governing body of the school has a responsibility for the development and approval of all the key policies within which the school functions. A prime task of governors is, therefore, to take an active part in the development of these policies. In this the governors will be working closely with the teaching staff of the school and, for certain topics, other school staff as well.

It is often helpful for individual governors to take a special responsibility for an area of the curriculum or the school's work. In doing this they are undertaking to develop a good working relationship with the subject co-ordinator or head of department. Where a new policy document is being developed in their area, the teacher responsible will probably prepare the draft and discuss it with the head teacher and the governor with that area of responsibility. When it is ready for presentation to the whole governing body the three key contributors, the teacher, the head and the governor, will agree how the document is to be presented and who will make the presentation. Should questions be asked at the Annual Parents' Meeting about a specialist area, it would be normal for the governor who takes an interest in that area to answer, with the head teacher providing any further depth that the question required. One of the governors must take on the role of governor for Special Educational Needs, another for child protection and another for issues arising from appraisal of staff.

As has been implied earlier, an important duty of governors is contributing to the network of communication without which no school can function. While all governors contribute to all aspects of this, there is a special expectation that governors will support and assist in the communication between the school and the body or group who nominated them.

Governors also have duties in the appointment of staff. These have been dealt with in some detail in the chapter on staff issues, but the principles are worth rehearsing here. The governors appoint the staff to the school or delegate that responsibility to others in clearly defined areas. Appointing the staff implies also accepting responsibility for their support, encouragement and professional development. It also implies accepting the responsibility for taking action if things have gone wrong. It is not adequate to argue that 'I wasn't a governor when Mrs Smith was appointed so it is nothing to do with me'. Governors have a corporate responsibility and, therefore, becoming a member of the governing body implies taking on the responsibility for previous decisions and policies.

It seems impossible not to mention money. School budgets loom very large in the management of the school. Governors are responsible for setting the school budget and monitoring its expenditure. The precise way in which these responsibilities are exercised will vary between different LEAs and will reflect their schemes for the fair funding of schools. Governors also have responsibility for other funds than those delegated to them by the LEA. All funds should be managed with openness and honesty and in accordance with good accounting practice. The National Society has developed a booklet of guidance on the management of charitable funds, about which those governors involved in financial matters should know.

Conduct of meetings

The chair of the governing body, the clerk and the head teacher will have discussed the agenda in good time before the meeting to ensure that it is well prepared. Preparation will include ensuring that the papers go out in good time before the meeting so that members of the governing body are able to consider the issues and prepare themselves for the discussion. The papers should also reach any adviser who will be present in good time, for the same reasons. There need to be special arrangements, known to all governors, for dealing with urgent business that arises after the agenda is prepared. Some items will appear regularly on every agenda, some will appear on an annual cycle and others only when they are needed. Some of the regular items include:

Prayer

Meetings of a Church school governing body should normally start with prayer. This will help to focus the meeting and remind all present that they are involved in work which is being done in the name of God. If there are individual members of the governing body who do not feel able to be present during prayers, arrangements should be made for them to join the meeting after the prayers have been said. It is important that the agenda makes it clear when the prayers will happen.

Election of chair

This is an annual item. In some years it may be no more than a formality, but it should be one of the most important decisions a governing body can make. In Church schools there has been a tradition that the parish priest is the chair of governors. This is only a tradition and in many schools the complex demands on governors have meant that it is no longer followed. The important principle is that the person best able to fulfil the role should be elected to the chair. The parish priest has many other contributions to make to the life of the school and it may be more appropriate for him or her to be freed from the responsibility of chairing meetings in order to take on these other roles more effectively.

Head teacher's report

This item will appear on the agenda of every meeting. The head teacher should present a written report and be prepared to answer questions on it. It is helpful if governors ask for items that they would like to see included in this report, to avoid the report falling into a routine pattern. It should not be used as means of raising items of substance that should have been on the main agenda. Where there are decisions to be taken by the governing body, it is helpful if these appear as separate items so that it is clear what is required. The report should be a report, not a separate mini-agenda.

Action Plans

Following an inspection, either by OFSTED (ESTYN in Wales) or under Section 23 of the Schools Inspection Act 1996, the governors must produce an Action Plan. Once the governing body has approved it, they should receive regular reports on its implementation, so that they can be sure that the school is making a full response to the inspection process. Governors must include an item on the progress of an Action Plan in their Annual Report to Parents.

Education Development Plans (EDPs)/ Education Strategic Plans (ESPs)

Every LEA must produce an Education Development Plan in consultation with local schools. It is intended that this should cover a three-year period but have provisions for an annual review. Within the plans there must be targets agreed with each school for the educational attainment of their pupils. The EDP will therefore be a regular item on the governors' agenda.

Asset Management Plans

Every LEA must have an Asset Management Plan. This is discussed in detail on page 95–6. The AMP and work related to it will be a regular feature of governing body agendas.

Items on admissions, finance, buildings, special educational needs, staffing and the curriculum will all be regular features of the agenda, but they have all been covered in some detail in other sections of the book.

The focus of this section has, so far, been on the formal structure of the meetings. This is because the meetings of the governing body are formal affairs and must be conducted properly. The business of the governors must be carried through effectively. There are other issues, however.

The formality of the meeting should not detract from the quality of the relationships which should exist between members of the governing body. In the chapters on parents and children, much emphasis was placed on the quality of relationships and the theological ideas that should inform them. Two groups of adults, the staff and the governors, are responsible for creating and maintaining these relationships. If relationships between members of these two groups do not demonstrate the principles that the school is seeking to promote, little of lasting value will be achieved.

The governors must ensure that every member of the governing body is encouraged to voice their opinion, contribute to debate and have their views acknowledged. This does not mean that the only way forward is total consensus. Nor does it give every individual a veto. It does mean that the chair should not cut short discussion until everyone has had ample opportunity to have his or her say. Having debated the issues and come to an agreement about them, all the governors should then accept the decisions of the majority and support them in public.

The preceding paragraph raises a further important issue, that of confidentiality. The details of the discussions in a governing body should remain confidential. Governors must know that what they say during a governors' meeting will not be repeated outside it. The minutes will record the decisions that have been taken. They should not record the detailed discussion. If governors are to have confidence in each other, they have to know that everyone present is observing these basic rules for committee work.

School policies

The governing body must approve a range of policies on which the school will depend for its good management. Some of these are required by law, others, although not statutory, are so important that inspectors and others concerned with the school's performance will ask to see them. Governors should not approve a policy that they do not understand; it is therefore important that governors read draft policies carefully, hear presentations on them from appropriate teaching or other staff and ask any questions that they may have before giving their approval. Once approved by the governing body, all governors should support the policy. They should also be satisfied that measures are in place to ensure that the policy is being implemented appropriately in the school.

First among these policies is the ethos statement that forms part of the Instrument of Government. From this statement the governors will have derived a mission statement or set of aims for the school. All other policies should relate to these basic statements of the purpose of the school. The policies, which the governors should consider for approval, will cover all the major areas of the curriculum and important aspects of the school's life as a community, such as discipline, security, pay for staff and delegation of financial responsibility.

Within every school there should be a scheduled process of policy review in order to ensure that no policy becomes out of date or ignored because it has not been discussed for a number of years. New staff and governors should be made aware of the key school policies as part of their induction programme.

Visiting the school

All governors, after due consultation with the head teacher, should seek to visit the school sufficiently regularly to be confident that they know something of its work. Some governors, because they also fulfil other roles in the life of the school, visit quite regularly and may make significant contributions in these other capacities. Governors should discuss plans for school visiting at least once a year as part of their agenda, in order to ensure that these visits are co-ordinated and do not become a burden to the school. It is good practice at the end of the visit for governors to discuss what they have seen with the head teacher or other senior member of staff in order to ensure that they have understood the context of their observations.

Training for governors

When a governor is first appointed to a school there should be a period of induction to enable him or her to take a full and informed part in the work of the governing body as quickly as possible. This may include:

- being given a folder of the key policies, documents and papers relating to the work of the governing body;
- making an informal visit to the school;
- meeting the head teacher;
- meeting the chair of the governors;

- being given a mentor from amongst the experienced governors.

Other training activities for governors take two basic forms.

- being part of a training activity organized for the whole governing body of the school;
- going on a course or conference as a representative of the governing body or from personal interest.

Over a period of time every governor will be involved in both types of training activity.

The main providers of training activities for governors are the LEAs, the dioceses and the associations of governors. They are also the main sources of advice to governors outside the staff of the school. Some governors may be interested in relating the training that they undertake to other forms of professional or personal development in which they are engaged. It is possible to find courses being offered to governors that have a clear relationship to validated programmes of study, leading to higher education qualifications in some areas. Your diocese or LEA will be able to provide details of these.

Within the school budget, or from other funds available to the school, governors should ensure that there is some funding available for their participation in training. Governors give up much free time to the service of the school. They should not also be expected to pay for their training out of their own pockets.

Finance

There are two distinct areas of finance for which the governors have responsibility. Each of the areas has its own rules and requires a particular type of response from the governing body.

'LMS' funds

The Local Education Authority delegates to all schools the funds that it is to use to cover the costs of the day to day running of the school. Each local authority has its own scheme, with accompanying regulations on how the scheme is to be operated in practice. These schemes must conform to guidelines laid down by the Department for Education and Employment and be approved by the department. The Local Education Authority must consult schools locally about changes that it proposes in its scheme. Governors have to develop policies related to the expenditure, such as a staff pay policy, and see that these are implemented. They should approve the annual budget and some governors may be involved in its development. The governors must also satisfy themselves that the budget is being managed efficiently in line with the policy and guidelines that they have approved. They must also ensure that all the areas of expenditure to be covered by the budget are properly identified. Where reserves are being built up against future large-scale expenditure, governors must ensure that this is being properly managed and that the reserves are only sufficiently large to cover the planned expenditure.

Governors' own funds

In Voluntary Aided and Foundation schools in particular, it is likely that the governors will have some funds that are their responsibility other than those delegated to them by the LEA. These funds may be the result of building appeals or the proceeds of letting the school buildings to third parties. Some governing bodies also benefit from trusts held in the name of the school. Some of these funds will be charitable and will therefore fall under the regime created by the Charities Acts. Detailed advice on the management of these funds is available in a National Society booklet on Church schools and charity law. The important principle to establish at this stage is that it is essential for the various funds to be kept separate and for movements between them to be carefully recorded. Governors have absolute responsibility for the money entrusted to them by the parents and supporters of the school and must be prepared to account for their use of the money to anyone with a legitimate reason for asking for the information.

External Relations

There is a wide range of groups within the local community and beyond with which the governing body of a Church school should maintain close working relationships. Many of these groups will appoint members to the governing body and those governors will naturally ensure that there are good channels of communication between the school and the body that appointed them. Locally, the principal groups will be the parents, the parish or parishes served by the school and the wider local community. The school brochure of information and any newsletter that the school publishes will be two of the ways in which communication is taken forward. How people are greeted when they visit the school or telephone the school office and their perception of how they are spoken to by the head teacher and the staff of the school will be very important.

Relationships with the Local Education Authority and the Diocesan Board of Education will be of a different nature. There will be a close professional relationship between the staff of the Local Education Authority, the Diocesan Board of Education and those who work most closely with them in the school. As always in a school, much will depend on the head teacher, but the chair of the governing body and those responsible for the school premises and finance will also have an important role in maintaining good relationships. The head teacher and those members of staff with curriculum responsibilities will know the advisory staff of the Local Authority and the Diocesan Board. The school secretary should maintain a list of the names and contact numbers of those within the Local Education Authority and the Diocesan Board of Education staff who are most often in contact with the school.

From time to time the school will come into contact with the local press, radio or television. This will often be because the school has some good news that it wishes to share or an event that it wishes to publicize. It is often helpful to have a member of staff or one of the governing body who maintains these links with the local media on behalf of the school, through whom such reports can be channelled. This will help to develop a good working relationship with local reporters, so that they know who to contact if they wish to discuss a school event or follow up a story. It also helps other staff and governors to know that there is a colleague who will answer questions on behalf of the school, so that they do not feel pressured into doing so. Indeed, if there is an event that needs delicate handling it is essential that only those with the authority of the governing body speak to the press on behalf of the school. In sensitive situations help should be sought from the media relations team of the Local Education Authority or Diocesan Communications Officer.

Management

Governors have a key role in the development of policy in the school and the appointment of the staff who will be responsible for the day to day management of the school. It is not the governors' task to manage the school. They can facilitate good management in the school by providing clear policies and being supportive of the head teacher and the school management team. Governors do have one important shared management task, however, which is to manage their own business and meetings effectively.

This chapter has outlined some of the main duties of the governing body. Being the member of a school governing body can be a daunting task but it is also a great privilege. Governors accept responsibility for everything that happens within a school, and are charged with ensuring that every pupil receives the best possible education.

For more information

- Connect to the churchschools.co.uk web site.
- Put in your password to access the welcome menu.
- Follow the link to Church School Management.
- Select the **governors** section using the button on the menu.

The **governors** section will open onscreen. Here you will find the text of this chapter together with links to more detailed information.

- Follow the links to the subsections that you need.

http://www.churchschools.co.uk

Curriculum Issues

Schools are about the education of children. Therefore what is learnt in schools is of vital importance to those who are charged with the management and governance of schools. This learning comes in two interrelated forms. First, there is the formal curriculum of the school, much of it set in a framework of legal requirements and national or local guidance. Secondly, there is what children and young people learn as a result of being part of the school community and participating in its life, rituals and pattern of relationships for several years. This second area is more often left to chance than the first and is less well defined. This chapter will explore some of the issues raised for Church schools by both types of learning. Every Church school must have an ethos statement as part of its Instrument of Government. This statement should sum up in a few words the basis on which the school was founded, on which the whole of the curriculum in both the senses used within this paragraph will be built. All ethos statements in Anglican schools should make clear that the school's life draws deeply on Anglican tradition and teaching.

The formal curriculum

Since 1988 the main content of the formal curriculum has been enshrined in law. The Education Reform Act of that year introduced two key curriculum concepts, the Basic Curriculum and the National Curriculum.

The Basic Curriculum is defined as Religious Education and those subjects that form the National Curriculum. Every school in the maintained system must provide at least the Basic Curriculum for all pupils of statutory school age.

The National Curriculum is defined as a particular set of ten subjects (eleven in Wales), whose content is laid down in syllabuses drawn up for the government by the Qualifications and Curriculum Authority (ACCAC in Wales).

The subjects within the Basic Curriculum share an important characteristic. The syllabuses for all the subjects are created externally to the school, except in some very limited cases. Governors and teachers working on reviews of school curriculum policies must therefore ensure that they know what the current syllabuses contain, and seek to ensure that, as far as possible, their own documentation reflects that content.

Religious Education

The source of the external syllabus for Religious Education varies according to the status of the school. For Community schools and others that do not have a religious character, it is always the LEA. For Voluntary Aided schools with a religious character the relevant diocese or denominational group may provide a syllabus or curriculum guidance. If there is no external guidance, governors in such schools have to take the full responsibility for ensuring that their syllabus for Religious Education fully reflects the traditions of their faith. In Voluntary Controlled or Foundation schools, Religious Education must be provided, where parents request it, in accordance with the religious character of the school. Where no such request is received, the syllabus is that produced by the LEA. Every LEA must have a current syllabus for Religious Education which has been developed or approved by the LEA Conference on Religious Education. This syllabus is known as the Agreed Syllabus. Support for the LEA syllabus is focused through the LEA Standing Advisory Council for Religious Education. In all schools parents have the right to withdraw their children from Religious Education.

The National Curriculum

Much has been written about the National Curriculum in the period since it was first introduced. Your school will have many documents laying out what is required at each Key Stage and Attainment level for each subject. The curriculum has already undergone a complete revision and a further revision is being prepared for the beginning of the new millennium. Perhaps the most contentious issue surrounding the National Curriculum is the amount of classroom time that it demands. It is supposed to be limited to 70 per cent of total teaching time. If this can be achieved, there is space to provide Religious Education with a reasonable allocation and also to have some material which is not in the prescribed curriculum but reflects the needs of the pupils in your particular area. Within the context of this short book there is no space to cover in more detail the range of issues that arise from the National Curriculum.

Personal Health and Social Education

This is one example of a curriculum topic for which some space needs to be found within the teaching time available in a school. Discussion continues among educationists about whether this topic is a curriculum subject in its own right or whether it is actually a cross-curricula issue drawing on contributions from most subject areas. If aspects of health education, sex education, careers education, parenting, drugs education, citizenship, safety and relationships are all to find an appropriate slot within this umbrella topic, then there will probably need to be a specific allocation of teaching time for it. Many of the elements within Personal Health and Social Education are of particular significance in a Church school. Governors will wish to ensure that the approaches adopted are informed by Christian insights and reflect the ethos statement of the school.

Sex Education

Sex Education must appear as part of the curriculum in secondary schools. Governors of primary schools may decide whether the school should make provision for sex education; if they decide that the school should not provide formal teaching on this subject they should provide their staff with clear guidance on how children's questions about it are to be answered. Parents have the right to withdraw their children from all aspects of sex education that are not required by the National Curriculum.

The hidden curriculum

This is a term that is sometimes used to describe those informal aspects of learning that occur simply because pupils are part of a school community. They learn about relationships, not by being taught or by discussing, but principally by experiencing the quality of relationships that exist within the school and within their home. They learn about values in the same way. They learn about the benefits of being good, and the problems that are caused when you are bad, through experience and observation within the community. This is powerful learning. It is learning from every adult involved in the school and from each other. It is very important that the adults who are responsible for the governance and management of the school understand the need to develop clear policies in these areas and take action to ensure that they are followed. The 'hidden curriculum' should not be hidden from teachers and governors.

Spiritual, Moral, Social and Cultural Education

Alongside the National Curriculum, the Education Reform Act 1988 made it clear that schools had a responsibility for the Spiritual, Moral, Social and Cultural Development of their pupils.

Since 1988 much time and energy has been expended by educationists on attempts to produce satisfactory definitions and guidance for teachers of these four ideas, particularly the first two. The National Society has published a series of booklets on these topics, which deal with issues in great detail. Every Church school should have copies of these booklets available and have incorporated some of their insights into the school's policy documents.

School worship

The programme of worship in the school will make a significant contribution to the ethos of the school, the hidden curriculum and the Spiritual, Moral, Social and Cultural development of the children in the school. The policy on which the programme of worship will be built will be based on the richness and diversity of the Anglican tradition of worship, while paying proper attention to the traditions of the local parish and the age and maturity of the children. The National Society has published a wide range of material in support of school worship. Some of this is available in book form and some is available through the Society's web site.

Inspection

In Church schools there are two distinct elements to the inspection process. A jargon has grown up to distinguish them which is derived from the sections of the Schools Inspection Act 1996, which define them. Section 10 inspections are undertaken by teams appointed by OFSTED/ESTYN. These inspections cover all the aspects of a Church school that would be inspected in a Community school, which are not inspected under Section 23 inspections. A team led by a registered inspector carries out section 10 inspections. They follow the pattern for inspection laid out in the relevant phase handbook published by OFSTED/ESTYN. Under Section 23 of the Act the school governors appoint inspectors who inspect those aspects of the school which are conducted in accordance with the school's trust deed. The National Society has created a training scheme for these inspectors and over 90 per cent of all Section 23 inspections in Anglican schools are conducted by inspectors who have been on this course. Both inspections should normally be carried out in the same academic year. In both cases the governors receive the inspection report, which is a public document. The governors must respond to each report by producing an Action Plan and ensuring that the plan is carried out.

Section 23 inspections apply to all schools that have a religious character, but affect the various categories of school within this group differently. The following table shows how each category of school will normally be affected.

	Voluntary Aided	**Voluntary Controlled**	**Foundation**
Religious Education	Section 23	Section 10 (unless they teach denominational education)	Section 10 (unless they teach denominational education)
School Worship	Section 23	Section 23	Section 23
Spiritual, Moral, Social and Cultural Education	Section 23 & Section 10	Section 23 (if the governors ask for it) & Section 10	Section 23 (if the governors ask for it) & Section 10

Note: Section 10 inspectors will report on whether the school is complying with the law on school worship.

Every Anglican school should have a copy of the *Handbook on Inspection Under Section 23*, published by the National Society, as this provides clear and detailed guidance on what to expect from a Section 23 inspection in an Anglican school.

Parental concerns

Sometimes parents become concerned about an aspect of the teaching or the content of the curriculum. In the first instance they should discuss this with the class teacher or head of department. If they are not satisfied with the discussion, they should discuss the issue with the head teacher. Most issues are resolved at this stage. Occasionally the parent wishes to take the matter further. Their next step is to approach the governing body. Ideally this approach should be through the clerk. It is for the governing body to decide how they will handle the issue, but they should seek to do so in a way that takes seriously the issues that the parent has raised. They may decide to invite the parent to part of a meeting of the governing body so that they can present their concerns in person. They should certainly instruct the clerk to write to the parent after the meeting at which the concern has been discussed, communicating the governor's response. Governors should be aware that the parent then has rights of appeal to the LEA or the diocese, depending on the area of the curriculum about which the parent has been concerned.

If parents approach individual governors about their concerns, it is important that the governors encourage the parents to use the route laid out above. If it is has reached the stage when it needs to come to the governing body, the individual governor should put the parent in touch with the clerk. The governor should never seek to raise the matter themselves during a business meeting of the governors without having discussed it with the clerk and ensured that it has been appropriately placed on the agenda after proper preparation.

So far in this chapter little has been said about teaching methodology. The emphasis has been on curriculum policy, context and inspections. This is because methodology is almost entirely a matter of professional judgement for the teaching staff of the school. Issues of methodology will arise in the governing body in response either to inspection or to requests for significant expenditure on buildings or equipment to enable improved teaching strategies to be adopted. Naturally, governors will be interested in how pupils are taught, but they should expect to learn about this area as much through their school visits and their informal discussions with staff as through the business items on the governors agenda.

If pupils are to receive a good education in the school, governors will need to ensure that they give time and energy to discussion of curriculum issues.

For more information

- Connect to the churchschools.co.uk web site.
- Put in your password to access the welcome menu.
- Follow the link to Church School Management.
- Select the **curriculum** section using the button on the menu.

The **curriculum** section will open onscreen. Here you will find the text of this chapter together with links to more detailed information.

- Follow the links to the subsections that you need.

http://www.churchschools.co.uk

The Schools Themselves

Status

There are three types of Church school, each with its own characteristics. There are some features which all Church schools share which distinguish them from schools that do not have a religious foundation. In all Anglican schools:

- the school worship must relate to the Anglican tradition;
- trustees will own the school buildings (although there are some exceptions);
- governors control the use of the school premises outside school hours but there are some rights for the LEA (governors may transfer control to another body under certain limited circumstances);
- there must be staff able to teach Religious Education in accordance with an Anglican syllabus;
- anyone appointed to be head teacher in the future must be able, at the least, to demonstrate her or his ability to sustain and develop the Anglican character of the school.

In all these areas dioceses will be able to provide advice to governing bodies.

The strange choice of the words 'Voluntary Aided' and 'Voluntary Controlled' to describe the main categories of Church school in the Education Act 1944 has led to some confusion over the years.

- Church of England (Voluntary Aided) school does not mean a school aided by the Church, but one owned and managed by the Church 'aided' by the LEA and the DfEE/ Welsh Assembly.

- Church of England (Voluntary Controlled) school does not mean a school controlled by the Church of England. In these schools no single group of governors has control.

Two similar potential sources of confusion may arise after September 1999 as a result of the School Standards and Framework Act.

- The first is between 'Foundation schools' and 'Foundation governors'. In all Church schools there are foundation governors who are nominated by various Church bodies. Anglican Church schools are owned by trustees who do not necessarily appoint governors directly. In Foundation schools without a religious character there is a Foundation which owns the school and this Foundation nominates the foundation governors for these schools.
- The second potential confusion is between schools of any category that deliberately set out to make their facilities available to the local community and the category of schools known as 'Community schools'. The name of this latter group of schools is designed to indicate that they are owned by the Local Education Authority and managed by governors representing the local community. It does not indicate that they are necessarily any more committed to serving their local community than schools of any other category.

The following tables summarize the differences between the three different types of Church schools.

	Voluntary Aided schools	Voluntary Controlled schools	Foundation schools
Buildings	Owned by trustees: The trust deed determines basis on which the school is run. New building and external repairs are the responsibility of the governors (supported by grant from the Department for Education and Employment up to 85% of approved expenditure). Playing fields are provided by the LEA.	Owned by trustees. The trust deed determines how the school shall be run where the law does not make this clear. All replacement, repairs and other building costs fall on the LEA.	Owned by trustees. The trust deed determines the basis on which the school shall be run where the law is silent. Playing fields owned by governors. All building works funded from LEA.
Staff a) Teaching	Employed by the governors, paid by the LEA. Governors may seek evidence of Christian commitment from applications for teaching posts.	Appointed by the governors, employed and paid by the LEA. Governors are bound by LEA appointing policies. Governors will be able to satisfy themselves that a candidate for the post of head teacher is suitable to support and develop the ethos of a Voluntary Controlled school.	Employed by the governors, paid by the LEA. Governors will be able to select teachers within the LEA policy. Governors are bound by LEA appointing policies. Governors will be able to satisfy themselves that a candidate for the post of head teacher is suitable to support and develop the ethos of a Foundation school.

Staff b) Support	Employed either by governors or contractors. If employed by governors they are paid by LEA.	Employed either by LEA or contractors. LEA employees usually appointed by governors.	Employed either by governors or contractors. If employed by governors they are paid by LEA.
Worship	Reflects the Anglican tradition and can include worship in the parish church.	Reflects the Anglican tradition and can include worship in the parish church.	Reflects Anglican tradition and can include worship in the parish church.
RE	Governors determine a syllabus that reflects the Anglican traditions. They may make use of the diocesan syllabus where this exists.	The school must follow the LEA syllabus unless the parents request a denominational one. The foundation governors have rights in the appointment of staff (called reserved teachers) to teach denominational Religious Education.	The school must follow the LEA syllabus unless the parents request a denominational one. The foundation governors have rights in the appointment of staff (called reserved teachers) to teach denominational Religious Education.
Membership of the governing body	Church (foundation) governors have an absolute majority over all other governors. Parish priest usually *ex officio* a member of the governing body. All governors combine to elect the chair. A proportion of foundation governors must also be parents.	Church (foundation) governors are in a minority. The parish priest is usually *ex officio* a member of the governing body. All governors combine to elect the chair.	Church (foundation) governors are in a minority. The parish priest is usually *ex officio* a member of the governing body. All governors combine to elect the chair.

Funding	LEA LMS formula. Governors' costs for building work from locally raised funds, PCCs, local trusts and, usually, trusts administered by the dioceses.	LEA LMS formula.	LEA LMS formula.
Admissions	Governors determine the policy and make the decisions. They must consult the LEA each year.	The LEA is responsible for admissions, but must consult the governing body each year.	Governors determine the policy and make the decisions. They must consult the LEA each year.
Advice	LEA Chief Education Officer has certain rights to attend governor meetings to give advice. Diocesan Directors of Education have parallel rights.	LEA Chief Education Officer has certain rights to attend governor meetings to give advice. Governors may give similar rights to the Diocesan Director of Education.	LEA Chief Education Officer has certain rights to attend governor meetings to give advice. Governors may give similar rights to the Diocesan Director of Education.
Inspection	OFSTED/ESTYN inspectors look at most issues. Section 23 inspectors inspect RE, worship and school ethos.	OFSTED/ESTYN inspectors look at general issues and RE. Section 23 inspectors inspect worship and may report on ethos.	OFSTED/ESTYN inspectors look at general issues and RE. Section 23 inspectors inspect worship and may report on ethos.

Notes on the tables:

Voluntary Aided

In these schools the Church has a majority of the governors. This should make it possible for there to be clear Christian leadership in all areas of the conduct of the school. This will depend, however, on the extent to which the governors are able to establish and maintain a policy for the appointment of teachers that ensures sufficient numbers of teachers with a strong Christian faith.

Voluntary Controlled and Foundation schools

There are many that argue that the balance on the governing body between the various groups who nominate governors mirrors the partnerships that should exist within a Church school. The fact that there is no group with a majority on the governing body can be an incentive to ensure that the school moves forward through consensus.

Buildings

While trustees own the buildings it is for the governors to ensure that they are well maintained and improved where and when necessary. How this work is funded depends on the status of the school (see preceding sections). The principles, however, are the same for all schools:

- Schools must be safe places for staff and pupils to work and for parents and others to visit.
- Maintenance delayed creates larger bills later.
- All work should be undertaken within the framework created by the Asset Management Plan (AMP) for the school.
- A qualified architect or surveyor should supervise major repair work and all improvements; usually this person or

their organization will develop a long-term working relationship with the governing body.

- If volunteers are used to carry out some of the tasks, their work should be supervised by someone who is professionally competent and care should be taken to ensure that the work is completed to the highest possible standard.
- When an outside contractor is employed to undertake work on a school building, the firm should be competent to do the work and carry appropriate insurance.

In one of the points above reference was made to the Asset Management Plan. The LEA will have produced an Asset Management Plan for all the school buildings in its area. The governors of each school need to use this basic information to produce their own plan for their school. This plan will identify a schedule for recurring maintenance, such as external redecoration, and an outline of how the school buildings might be developed to ensure that they provide the best possible environment in which to educate the pupils. The LEA Asset Management Plan will consider issues of the building's state of repair, its ability to accommodate the number of pupils now on roll or expected in the future and the suitability of the teaching and other facilities for their task. The Asset Management Plan for the school should reflect the same priorities.

The existence of a LEA Asset Management Plan is designed to ensure that government grants are targeted to those schools in greatest need.

Insurance

All schools need to carry a range of insurance cover. Most of this is provided or arranged through Local Education Authorities. Schools need to be satisfied that they have a clear understanding of what insurance the LEA provides.

Governors of Voluntary Aided schools are advised to have their own insurance for those aspects of the buildings for which they have responsibility. This is usually arranged through the diocese as a block policy. One or two LEAs arrange this cover for their schools.

Governors of all Church schools are also advised to ensure that they have a public liability policy related to the use that they have of the building. This is usually organized through the diocese as a block policy. Governors of Aided and Foundation schools have additional responsibilities as employers of staff. They are advised to ensure that they have a legal liability insurance to cover any issues that may arise from these duties. Most dioceses have made appropriate arrangements for their schools in this area. Insurance for schools is an area of rapid change and development. Before making any changes to their policies governors or school managers should discuss the issues with their diocese or LEA.

Change of Status

Occasionally it may be appropriate for schools to consider whether they have the most appropriate status for their circumstances. Schools cannot change status too often. Currently, once a change has been made they must wait five years before considering a further change. This means, for example, that no former Grant Maintained school which adopted a new status on 1 September 1999 can make a further change before 1 September 2004.

Any school considering a change of status should consult their Diocesan Director of Education at the earliest possible opportunity.

The following changes are possible after 1 September 2000.

Voluntary Controlled to Voluntary Aided status

There are a number of schools who have expressed interest in this change. This is to be expected because, until the passage of the

School Standards and Framework Act 1998, this was the most difficult change to make. It is now rather easier and therefore there are some schools who would like to make the change and for whom it would now be possible for the first time. These are schools where the LEA has spent significant sums on the buildings of the school since it became a Controlled school.

Since 1986 the change from Controlled to Aided was only possible if the governors compensated the LEA for the full amount they had spent on improving, extending, remodelling or replacing the building. No grant was available from the DfEE/Welsh Office for this purpose. This compensation is still payable, but only if the school closes, when the LEA will have a claim against the proceeds of the sale of the school.

The procedure for change of status involves local consultation, the issuing of public notices and approval by the Secretary of State/Welsh Assembly. He will require evidence that the governors can, with appropriate support, meet the financial obligations of Voluntary Aided status. It will be clear that this change is unlikely to be effected without the active support and involvement of the diocese.

Voluntary Aided to Voluntary Controlled status

The arrangements for this move are unchanged by the 1998 Act. Governors can resolve to seek Voluntary Controlled status, but they have to do so at two separate meetings and they must have consulted the Diocesan Director of Education between the meetings. This is to ensure that they are aware of what support is available to them. In the period between the 1980s and 1944 it was possible for governors to make the move at a single meeting. Some governors did so when faced with a significant bill for repairs or improvements, apparently unaware of the help that was available to them from their diocese. Given the ease with which this change could be made in the past it is not likely that it will be an appropriate move for many Aided schools in the next few years.

Voluntary Controlled to Foundation status

This may be an attractive move for some schools, but much depends on the way in which Foundation schools fit into the education service in the next few years. Most governors will wish to be cautious about making this change when the existence of Foundation schools in the system is still recent. The same comments apply to the move from Voluntary Aided to Foundation status.

Other moves

Moves from Foundation status will not be possible under current law before 1 September 2004. Governors considering such a move should explore the advantages and disadvantages nearer that time in consultation with their diocese.

No Church school can move to Community status. This involves a total closure of the school. The LEA would then have to purchase the building and open a new school in the premises.

Finance

The early chapter on governors provided an introduction to some of the financial issues that concern governors and school managers. In this section the focus is on the financial implications of the school buildings. In Voluntary Aided schools the governors must be prepared to find at least 15 per cent of the cost of work on the buildings that are their responsibility. They are supported in this by the Diocesan Board of Education and may sometimes be able to draw upon trust funds held for the purpose of supporting Voluntary Aided schools. The governors must also insure their building and users of the building on those occasions when they give permission for it to be used for purposes other than the provision of education within the orbit of the Local Education Authority. Any income gained from these lettings, after payment into the school's LMS funds of any costs incurred against that budget, is available to the governors to use to support their work and responsibilities.

This chapter has focused on issues that can seem remote from the education of children. Governors and school managers need to ensure that they have addressed the issues properly so that they have appropriate solutions for their school. If the status and buildings are right, all the energy can be focused on the quality of education. Where they are wrong they raise issues that dominate people's agenda and distract from concern for the needs of the pupils.

For more information

- Connect to the churchschools.co.uk web site.
- Put in your password to access the welcome menu.
- Follow the link to Church School Management.
- Select the **school** section using the button on the menu.

The **school** section will open onscreen. Here you will find the text of this chapter together with links to more detailed information.

- Follow the links to the subsections that you need.

http://www.churchschools.co.uk

The Civil Framework for Church Schools: National and Local Government

The context within which Church schools operate is created by a partnership between local and national government and the Churches at local and national level. This chapter will explore the government aspects of that partnership and the following chapter will deal with the Church dimension. Those involved in leading Church schools need to be aware of the way in which the various agencies locally and nationally work together and share responsibilities. This is important in order to understand how the work of their individual school relates to these partnerships and where they can best turn for help and support in particular circumstances.

National government

The role of national government and its agencies is to create the overall framework for schools, set standards, provide effective support and monitoring and ensure that there is a high-quality flow of recruits into the teaching profession. In recent years it has also taken responsibility for setting standards for professional development for teachers. It achieves these tasks through legislation and the work of government departments and agencies.

The framework

The major legislation which affects schools is contained in the Education Acts of 1996 and the School Standards and

Framework Act 1998. The 1996 Acts consolidated education law passed between 1944 and 1995; thus, although there have been many changes, much of the education system that we have inherited owes its origins to an Education Act passed in wartime. It is remarkable that, despite the pressures of wartime, the 1944 Act was only passed after a considerable period of consultation and following considerable negotiations between government and the Churches. The principles established in 1944 have continued to inform the way in which education in this country has developed ever since. Education law requires that all children should receive a period of formal education between the ages of 5 and 16. Increasingly, provision is made for younger children to receive some education appropriate to their age if their parents wish them to participate. Similarly, many young people choose to stay on at school or in further education beyond the statutory school age of 16. The law does not require schools to serve defined age groups and since 1944 a mixed pattern of provision has grown up in different parts of the country, reflecting the decisions taken within particular Local Education Authorities (LEAs). Broadly speaking, however, there are three bands into which the statutory provision of education is divided:

- Primary, which is understood to encompass all education up to the end of the academic year in which the child reaches the age of 11;
- Secondary, which encompasses the rest of a young person's schooling, whether this ends at 16 or 18;
- Tertiary, which covers education offered in further education colleges and higher education colleges or universities.

Primary and secondary education are the responsibility of Local Education Authorities; tertiary education is funded through funding councils and organized on a national basis. In some parts of the country, schools are not separated into distinctively primary and secondary but include an intermediate or middle school stage. The advent of the National Curriculum introduced after the Education Reform Act of 1988, which provided a curriculum structure of Key Stages, two corresponding to the primary phase and two to the secondary, has created a new pressure which is leading some authorities to review the future of middle schools. Broadly speaking, the division into primary, secondary and tertiary has existed since 1944. The School Standards and Framework Act 1998, while not changing these broad bands, did provide for changes in the status of schools which affect the way in which they are governed and the responsibilities of individual governing bodies. There are three broad statuses for schools, regardless of whether they are primary schools, secondary schools or serving an age group within or across these two broad bands. The statuses are Community school, Foundation school and Voluntary school. Within the Voluntary status there are sub-divisions into Voluntary Aided and Voluntary Controlled. Details of the major difference between these types of school were given in the previous chapter.

The government agencies

At present the government has two main agencies that have an impact on what is taught in schools. As its name implies, the Qualifications and Curriculum Authority has a responsibility for the public examinations which are taken by pupils in schools as a measure of their progress at the ages of 7, 11 and 14 and to gain formal qualifications either at GCSE or A level at 16 and 18. It is also responsible for advising government on the content of the National Curriculum subjects and for providing support materials that show how the non-statutory subjects can interrelate with content that is required by law. The only exception to this framework is Religious Education which, because it has been a statutory requirement for far longer than the National Curriculum subjects, has the content of the curriculum determined locally rather than nationally. The Qualifications and Curriculum Authority has provided materials for Religious Education which are intended to be a resource for the local authority conferences which have responsibility for the subject.

The other agency involved in curriculum issues is the Office for Standards in Education (OFSTED) which is responsible for the inspection of all schools in England and for providing advice to government on the development of education, based on its inspection evidence. In Wales these duties are carried out by ESTYN, formerly known as the Office of Her Majesty's Chief Inspector (OHMCI). In Church schools OFSTED/ESTYN does not have complete responsibility. Those aspects of education which are determined by the school's trust deed are not inspected by an OFSTED/ESTYN appointed inspector but by one appointed by the governors as a fit person to inspect the denominational aspects of the school. The National Society has provided a national training scheme and framework for the inspection of Anglican schools (see next chapter for details).

The third major government agency intimately involved with schools is the Teacher Training Agency. The task of this agency is to ensure that there is a steady supply of high-quality, well-trained entrants into the teaching profession. In order to achieve this, it takes initiatives designed to encourage recruitment to the profession, sets standards for the training of new entrants and promotes a variety of routes into the profession and ways in which this training can be delivered. At present the responsibility for setting standards for the further professional development of teachers after qualification lies with the Department for Education and Employment itself, although it is the government's stated intention to transfer this responsibility to a National College for School Leadership during 2001. The programmes that are currently sustained and which will ultimately form part of the brief of the college are training for subject leaders, a National

Professional Qualification for Head teachers (NPQH), an induction programme for newly appointed head teachers, currently called 'Headlamp', and a Leadership Programme for Serving Head teachers (LPSH). Details of how these programmes are developing and how they can meet the needs of those exercising these different levels of responsibility within Church schools can be found on the National Society's web site.

At present the DfEE/Welsh Assembly are in the process of creating separate General Teaching Councils for England and for Wales. These will have rather different responsibilities and full details of them, as they affect Church schools, will be placed on the web site.

The Department for Education and Employment/Welsh Assembly not only set standards for schools through the work of their agencies; they also set standards for Local Education Authorities and, working with their agencies, undertake monitoring and inspection of the work of LEAs and scrutiny of some of their major schemes and policies.

Local Education Authorities

The Local Education Authority is responsible for providing the funding for schools in their area from council tax or from the money allocated to them from central government. While the authority may retain some funds for work designed to administer the system and support the development of high-quality education within their schools, the majority of the funding is delegated directly to the governing body of each school. This should enable schools to make budget decisions in ways that most directly benefit the education of the pupils in their school. The Local Education Authorities' responsibilities are not limited to financial affairs. They have to provide a number of services designed to meet the needs of individual pupils and a range of policy documents intended to set appropriate local standards and ensure that these are delivered. In their relationships with schools LEAs must operate within a centrally developed code of practice. In order to work with their schools and others concerned with education, the Local Education Authority will create a number of forums, committee and other meetings. Among the most important, in terms of their impact on Church schools, are the following.

The Education Committee or Education Scrutiny Committee

These two possible titles should be taken to indicate a description of the work of the committee within the structure of local government adopted by the local authority. The actual committee which covers this work may have a different title. The majority of members of this committee will be elected councillors but there will be members with full voting rights from the Churches and the parent body. Teachers may also have representation on the committee but without the right to vote.

School Organization Committees (SOC)

This committee brings together the various groups interested in school organization at local level and provides a forum in which the Local Education Authority's plans for the development of schools in its area can be discussed and, if the committee is so minded, approved. The main issues which will come to a School Organization Committee are authority plans for the reorganization of schools, school closures or the creation of new schools to meet the demand for more places. There are no School Organization Committees in Wales; the Local Education Authorities undertake their duties.

Standing Advisory Council for Religious Education (SACRE)

This council brings together those bodies in the authority with a particular interest in Religious Education and school worship. It has the responsibility for advising the Local Education Authority on these issues and taking initiatives to promote Religious Education and school worship in the area. It has a particular interest in the use of the Local Education Authority's Agreed Syllabus for Religious Education and a duty to inform the Local Education Authority if the syllabus needs revision. It does not have responsibility for Religious Education and school worship where these are undertaken in Church schools in accordance with the school's trust deed.

Agreed Syllabus Conference

If the Local Education Authority decides that its Agreed Syllabus for Religious Education needs revision, it must convene a conference for this purpose. The constitution of this Agreed Syllabus Conference is different from that of a Standing Advisory Council for Religious Education because there can be no co-opted members. Despite this difference, in many authorities the membership of the two bodies is almost identical. The conference only exists for the period of time that it takes to generate a new Religious Education syllabus for the authority and for this to receive approval by the Education Committee and the local authority.

Early Years Partnerships

These bring together all the parties concerned or involved with the provision of education for children up to the age of 14. They are charged with the responsibility of advising the authority on the best strategies to ensure that there are an adequate number of places for children whose parents wish them to have education before they reach statutory school age.

Admissions Forum

The Local Education Authority may bring together representatives of all those bodies involved in school admissions in order to discuss the co-ordination and administration of school admission and transfer between schools at whatever age this takes place. As well as the local authorities and the Churches, there will be representatives of Voluntary Aided and Foundation schools on the Admissions Forum because the governing bodies in these schools are the admission authority for the school. In some areas, neighbouring Local Education Authorities may also be represented on the admissions forum where there is a significant number of cross-border admissions.

A prime duty of the Local Education Authority is to act for school improvement and therefore much of the work that they do with schools and the services that they provide has this objective in mind.

European institutions

The European Union and the Council of Europe both have interests in education throughout the areas that they cover. They have particular interests in maintaining a European-wide standard on human rights, in particular the rights of a child, and to this end they promote European understanding, programmes of learning and visits. Many Church schools, both at primary and secondary level, are becoming involved in such programmes.

Organizations and associations of teachers

These fall into two distinct categories. The first is professional associations concerned with issues related to employment and professional responsibilities and duties. Most teachers belong to one of these professional associations and teachers can consult local and regional representatives over issues of concern. At the school level, representatives of these associations should be facilitated in carrying out their tasks on behalf of their members.

The other form of professional association of teachers is those that bring together teachers with a particular subject or phase interest. Some of these associations have a national structure and standing and make a major contribution to the continuing development of their subject or phase. Other groupings have a more local nature and serve as a forum for local professional development and curriculum action. This may be as simple as co-ordinating school sports fixtures and facilitating teams to represent the schools at LEA or regional level, or include such complex tasks as organizing national or international conferences for teachers with a particular interest and commitment to a single subject area. Many of these subject associations have come together at national level to create the College of Teachers, which exists to promote high standards of education and professional development amongst all members of the profession. Many Church schools benefit significantly from the participation of their teachers in such local or national associations.

For more information

- Connect to the churchschools.co.uk web site.
- Put in your password to access the welcome menu.
- Follow the link to Church School Management.
- Select the **State** section using the button on the menu.

The **State** section will open onscreen. Here you will find the text of this chapter together with links to more detailed information.

- Follow the links to the subsections that you need.

http://www.churchschools.co.uk

The Ecclesiastical Framework for Church Schools: the Local and National Church

In the previous chapter some of the framework of national and local government was outlined insofar as it affects the work of Church schools. Church schools not only relate to national and local government, they also have an important relationship with the Church by which they were established and whose practice and traditions of education they have a duty to reflect.

The Church locally

The support for education in the Church of England and the Church in Wales is organized locally at three distinct but complementary levels.

The local parish

The Anglican Church is based on a parochial system that covers the entire country. Each parish has a distinctive geographical boundary and the parish priest is given responsibility by the Church for the population within that boundary. The parish priest also has a number of responsibilities with regard to arrangements for Anglican worship and the supervision of the use of Anglican buildings within the parish. In every parish there is a Parochial Church Council and a number of churchwardens. Should there be a vacancy for a parish priest, the churchwardens automatically take over a number of the parish priest's responsibilities. Historically, when Anglican schools were founded the trustees of the building were often the parish priest and churchwardens of the parish in which the school was situated. Many of the more modern schools now have trust deeds which mention the diocese as the trustee of the school, but where the school was founded in the nineteenth century the trustees were either named individuals or, more usually, the holders of the major parochial offices.

The Parochial Church Council usually has the responsibility for nominating a proportion of the Church governors on the governing body. It may decide to include the head teacher of the school in its own membership. Where such arrangements have been established, it can be a sign of good mutual collaboration and confidence between the school and the parish in which it is set. Sometimes, as a result of historic agreements possibly deriving from school reorganization or the closure of neighbouring schools, other local Parochial Church Councils also nominate governors on to the governing body of a Church school.

The deanery

The next level of organization beyond the parish is the deanery. The deanery is led by a Rural or Area Dean who is usually one of the senior parochial clergy in the area, chosen by the Bishop after consultation with the other clergy of the area. The deanery also brings together elected members representing each of the Anglican churches in the deanery to a meeting known as a deanery synod in England and a deanery conference in Wales. Because of the wide area that they serve, a few Anglican secondary schools in England are closely related to the deanery and the deanery synod for the area. In such cases the deanery synod is likely to have the responsibility for nominating some of the Church governors.

The diocese in England

Beyond the deanery is the diocese, which is led by the diocesan bishop. There is also a body of elected representatives of the

Church called the Diocesan Synod, which exists to advise the bishop and be responsible for diocesan finances. Under the Diocesan Boards of Education Measure of 1991, every diocese in England is required to have a Diocesan Board of Education with a Diocesan Director of Education as its principal officer. This committee has a number of responsibilities in respect of the Church's involvement in statutory education and in particular its support for Anglican schools and for Religious Education and school worship in all schools. The Diocesan Board of Education may well employ specialist staff, as well as the Diocesan Director of Education, to support and help Church schools in matters of building, curriculum and school management. This team of people provides a very important source of support for Church schools in addition to that available from the Local Education Authority. Normally, very close working relationships exist between the Local Education Authority and the Diocesan Board of Education. The Diocesan Director of Education and other members of the diocesan education team are responsible to the Diocesan Board of Education for the work that they do on its behalf. The Diocesan Board of Education must make a report to the Diocesan Synod of the work it has undertaken on behalf of the diocese. For the most part the relationship between the Diocesan Director of Education, the Diocesan Board of Education and individual Church schools is a matter of advice and co-operation. Under certain limited circumstances the Diocesan Board of Education can give direction to a particular governing body if it believes the governing body is acting against the interests of its own Church school or all Church schools in general. There are clearly defined circumstances in which this power can be used and if the Diocesan Board of Education decides to use it, it must report what it has done to the Diocesan Synod.

Every Diocesan Board of Education sets its own priorities and responds to the needs of the schools in its area in ways which most closely reflect their needs and the limits of the resources that are available. Many Diocesan Boards of Education provide training for governors and senior staff of Church schools and for RE and worship co-ordinators in all schools. Some Diocesan Boards of Education provide Religious Education centres open to all interested teachers. The responsibilities of Diocesan Boards of Education are usually not limited to schools; they often include the Church's work in further and higher education and may extend to the Church's educational work in the parishes. This last area of work may fall under one of the other boards, councils or committees of the Diocesan Synod, if it has not been felt appropriate to include it within the brief of the Diocesan Board of Education.

The diocese in Wales

In Wales, the Diocesan Boards are known as Diocesan Councils for Education and through the Diocesan Directors of Education and their teams they offer support to the schools in much the same way as their counterparts in England.

The diocesan bishop is responsible for Church schools in the diocese and he delegates the discharge of that responsibility to the Diocesan Director of Education.

General

It is important for all Church schools to seek to maintain good relationships with the Diocesan Director of Education and the diocesan education team and it would be very surprising if there was an Anglican school which did not have a well-established pattern of contact with their local diocese. If issues about the nature of worship in Anglican schools or of Religious Education in Anglican Voluntary Aided schools arise within the school's staff, governing body or parents, the source of advice and guidance and the person to whom appeals can be made and who can decide on complaints related to these issues is the diocesan bishop. In most dioceses, however, the bishop would expect the issues to be referred to the Diocesan Director of Education in the first instance. The Diocesan Director will ensure that there is a sufficient level of support material in these particular areas of Anglican school work to provide a clear basis for guidance to schools. The endorsement of this guidance by the diocesan bishop is a strong indication of the view that he is likely to take, if appealed to for a decision on any issue in the above areas.

The Church nationally

Beyond the diocese the Church is organized in provinces, which are groups of dioceses under the leadership of an archbishop. There is, therefore, a province of Wales and, in England, provinces of York and Canterbury. In England much of the national work is carried out by the General Synod, which brings together representatives of both English provinces, and by the Archbishops' Council, which has responsibility for the direction of the Church's national work. Reporting to the Archbishops' Council is the Church of England Board of Education, which has the responsibility for representing the Church at national level in matters of education. One of its principle tasks on behalf of Church schools is to represent their interests nationally, particularly with the Department for Education and Employment at times of education legislation. The Church of England Board of Education is responsible for developing policy that has been approved by the Archbishops' Council and the General Synod. The education policy of the Church in Wales is developed in consultation between the Diocesan Directors of Education and the bench of bishops.

The National Society

The educational work of the Anglican Church in the provinces of England and Wales benefits from the support of the National

Society. This Anglican charity was founded in 1811 for the purpose of promoting Church schools. Its full name, according to the most recent of its royal charters, is the National Society (Church of England) for the Promotion of Religious Education. As it was the first national society for any purpose to be granted a royal charter, it has the privilege of being able to be known simply as the National Society. The Society works very closely with the Church of England Board of Education and the Church in Wales to support the work of Church schools and Religious Education, school worship and spiritual, moral, social and cultural development in all schools. It does this through publications, through courses offered in collaboration with the Church Colleges of Higher Education, through managing the Section 23 Inspection process in Anglican schools and through providing Religious Education centres of national standing in London and York. Many of the senior officers of the National Society are joint appointments with the Church of England Board of Education. Among the most recent developments sponsored by the National Society in support of Church schools is the development of the specialist web site for Church school management to which this short book is an introduction.

For more information

- Connect to the churchschools.co.uk web site.
- Put in your password to access the welcome menu.
- Follow the link to Church School Management.
- Select the **Church** section using the button on the menu.

The **Church** section will open onscreen. Here you will find the text of this chapter together with links to more detailed information.

- Follow the links to the subsections that you need.

http://www.churchschools.co.uk

Welcome to the Church Schools Web Site

All the issues in this book are considered in more detail in the Church school management section of the National Society's churchschools.co.uk web site.

In order to gain access to the Church schools management section of the web site you will need a password. You can obtain this in two ways. You can take out a personal subscription, or, if you work in or are a governor of a school that has a subscription, you may use the school password. If you are a student on a course leading to qualified teacher status, you will probably find that your college has arranged for access to the site through the college computer facilities.

The address of the site is http://www.churchschools.co.uk.

When you first reach the site you will be asked to type in your password to gain access, or to register if you have not yet paid a subscription. The first time you enter the site you should read the introductory pages, which will explain how you can find your way into the various sections and how you can make use of the resources that are available for you to print out and use.

The Church schools management section of the web site is organized into the same chapters as this book. Therefore, if you need more information about a topic mentioned in a chapter in this book, you should go to the sections of the site that has a name similar to the chapter heading. When the section opens up you will see a menu on the right-hand side of the screen. Following the links on the menu will take you to information on specific areas of interest. The information on each area will be organized under seven broad headings, which are as follows:

Issues for Church schools

This will identify specific ways, if any, in which Church schools will need to deal with the area in a different manner from other schools.

Guidance

This will provide direct guidance on the topic, based on legal advice and experience gathered from around the country.

Difficult areas

This will identify some of the areas where the law or general guidance seems unclear or uncertain, or where there is no experience on which to base guidance. It will include issues on which, because of their sensitive nature, personal advice should be sought from your diocese.

The law

This will give the references to the key sections of legislation for the topic in question.

Frequently asked questions

This will contain a list of short questions and answers on issues related to the topic, drawn from the experience of the National Society and Diocesan Officers.

Resources

This section will provide details of books and papers that relate to the topic. It will often include material that you can download and print off to use in your school.

Diocesan issues

These pages are of primary interest to members of diocesan education teams, but may also be read by anyone who wishes to browse.

In addition, in many areas of the site one or more of the following will appear:

Specific points for schools in Wales

Where the framework for Welsh schools differs from that for English schools, there will be a marker within the text of the site that will lead to an explanation of the difference.

Resources to print out

At a number of points within the site there will be links to resources designed for you to store in your school's computer and to use as part of your school's management or administration. These are also gathered together in a single resources section to enable you to access the material that you need quickly.

Links to other significant sites

Finding your way into the range of educational sites that are now available grows more complex as these sites proliferate. Wherever there is a useful site that can give more information, guidance or resources, you will find a direct link to that site, thus saving considerable time researching other services or 'surfing' the web to find them.

If, after searching the church schools.co.uk web site, you still cannot find the answer to your question, the site provides you with details and email links to members of the National Society's team so that you can contact the team member who is most likely to be able to help you.

At the time of writing plans exist for some 2,000 'pages' of information to be made available during the course of the year 2000. After that date the site will continue to be regularly revised and brought up to date in the light of changes to the law and developments in experience and good practice in church schools.

Church schools magazine online

In addition to the above there is a wealth of material for those involved in Church schools in our regularly updated online magazine, including:

- resources and features on Church school issues;
- RE and collective worship resources;
- regular features from Church schools, with head teachers and teachers giving practical advice in both primary and secondary situations;
- online forum for governors, head teachers and teachers;
- competitions, news and book reviews.

To open the magazine, follow the links to the Church schools magazine from the home page of churchschools.co.uk, or from the title page of the Church schools management section of the web site.

Index